ISBN 1-883733-17-0

Edited by Katie Supinsky

Cover design by Dolores Gillum, Kathexis Design

Global Insights Publishing
1302 Holm road
Petaluma, CA 94954, USA
(707) 763-8380 Fax (707) 763-3640

Measuring Diversity Results

Edward E. Hubbard, Ph.D.

Preface

INTRODUCTION

This book is about creating successful diversity initiatives and building a strategic advantage in organizations. Successful diversity initiatives rely on your ability to fully understand the organization's business, the nature of diverse work force personnel, the organization's strategic business objectives, its marketplace, the wisdom to spend your time on the issues which are important, and the skill to communicate your results.

If the language of business is dollars, then the alphabet is numbers. All organizations, whether profit or not-for-profit, depend on their ability to get the best possible return on dollars invested. Even some governmental agencies who thought they were immune from this basic law have found themselves severely cut back by an electorate which demands service in return for their tax dollars. In essence, the need for measurement and bottom-line results is inescapable.

What if you're making terrific progress and don't know it?

METHODS USED IN THIS BOOK

The diversity measurement approach used in this book is both experiential and practical. There are a number of excellent books on diversity in organizations, many covering various aspects of diversity and even more books on the fundamentals of statistics and measurement. Therefore, I have included little reference to theory and even less to statistics. Although we will deal with numbers throughout the book, the mathematics are very basic. The four functions of arithmetic will take care of 99 percent of the applications covered.

This material is meant to be a conversation between you and me about the subject of diversity measurement, therefore, my style is intended to be familiar and somewhat informal. I want to discuss some of the key issues I see in diversity measurement and provide you with a few ideas on how to deal with them. This book is intended to be a step-by-step, how-to method to help you measure diversity results.

If you are involved with designing and implementing a diverse work environment or culture in any way, you will want to read this book

You may find that this book represents one of the most comprehensive text on the subject available today. It provides a starter kit of tools to help you build the structure necessary to achieve your diversity initiatives and assist the organization in meeting its strategic business objectives. These tools should be used selectively in that this book is not a panacea. Everyone's environment is somewhat unique. My purpose is to explain where and how to use each tool, allowing you the opportunity to select which formulas and methods best apply to your organization's needs.

A map of the book's chapter structure is included in chapter one in the section entitled: "When and How To Use This Book." Measures in this book are designed around an organizational change and systems construct called the Diversity 9-S Framework. It can provide an enhanced view of the requirements for comprehensive change to an inclusive, diversity friendly work environment that centers on the strategic business needs of an organization. The book's chapter map is designed to make it easy to locate information.

The trend towards accountability and measurement in diversity is probably the most significant development in the diversity field in recent years. Yet, some diversity professionals are reluctant to change their approach. Many would like to include measurement as part of their strategy but simply don't know how. Other practitioners understand and want to use measurement however few measures exist.

In short, numbers drive the business

Based upon my client work and discussions with colleagues in the diversity field, there appeared to be a void unfilled. That's why I wrote this book.

I hope that it will make it easier for diversity professionals to apply practical and innovative solutions to the paradoxical challenges faced by Diversity change efforts. Diversity is often viewed as a "soft" and sometimes unclear contributor to the organization's performance and bottom-line, yet its potential, if understood, could generate a wealth of resources for improved performance and enhance dollar return-on-investment.

I hope you will find this book to be an invaluable resource and a systematic process to measure diversity results from a practical point of view.

Acknowledgments

My first and deepest appreciation must go to my beautiful wife, best friend and partner, Myra. Her love, caring, encouragement, and support provides the fuel and focus for my writing endeavors. This book is dedicated to you.

Secondly, I would like to thank my wonderful family. My loving, courageous mother, Geneva Hubbard, whose words of strength are my guiding light. My beautiful sisters and their families, Leona Butler, Lois Branch, Sylvia Johnson, Janice Bush, Deborah Richardson. Thank you from the bottom of my heart for all your support and many prayers. And to a host of other relatives...thank you.

There are a number of people, whether they know it or not, who made the completion of this book possible. Some of them provided their scholarly works. Others provided personal encouragement and detail conversations which enriched my thinking.

I am indebted to the many scholars on measurement such as Jac Fitz-enz, Saratoga Institute whose approach to measurement convinced me that measuring diversity results could be done in a practical way, Jack J. Phillips, Peter Bramley, Thomas Kramlinger, Ron Zemke, Donald Kirkpatrick, Wayne Casio, William Christopher, Carl Thor, Lyle Spencer, Richard Sloma, and others too numerous to mention.

Their thought-provoking research created foundation pathways and methods for crafting many of the initial diversity measures and processes.

To all of those who shared their experiences and knowledge on this subject such that others may learn and benefit.

I am indebted to a host of diversity professionals. Julie O'Mara, Kay Iwata, Juan Lopez, Price Cobbs, Francie Kendall, Steve Hanamura, Eric Hanamura, R. Roosevelt Thomas, Jeff Howard, Jay Lucus, Nancy DiTomaso, Mary Francis Winters, Bill Bean, Carol McHuron, Larry Baytos, Taylor Cox, Lynda White, Sid Reel, Sonny Massey, David Tulin, Lee Gardenswartz, Anita Rowe, the attendees at the September, 1995 Diversity 2000 Conference, participants in my diversity 9-S and measurement workshops, and others too numerous to name.

I am indebted to the late Gwen Jones and the evaluation staff of the Federal Aviation Administration for their ideas and information included in the Diversity Training Evaluation Toolkit.

To my editor and friend, Katie Supinsky, whose meticulous work helped me to shape this outcome.

To my NLP community of friends for their encouragement and processes which helped me develop the resources I needed to finish this book amidst a challenging schedule.

To Dolores Gillum of Kathexis Design for her insightful creative talent and design of the book dust jacket, re-creation of the Diversity 9-S Framework, and other illustrations. You really know your stuff!

And of course, to our tremendous Hubbard & Hubbard staff whose hard work and coordination brings the final touches together.

Acknowledgments

In any work such as this, there are many who have contributed that may get overlooked. Please forgive me if I missed you in this list. I thank you all.

Edward E. Hubbard
Petaluma, California

MEASURING DIVERSITY RESULTS

Contents

PREFACE iii
    Introduction iii
    Methods Used in this Book iii
    Acknowledgments vii

CONTENTS xi

Chapter 1 INTRODUCTION 1
    Who Should Read This Book 1
    When and How To Use This Book 4

Chapter 2 YOU CAN'T MEASURE WHAT WE DO IN DIVERSITY WORK...CAN YOU?? 7
    It's All Subjective 7
    Reasons Why Not 10
    Actions Speak Louder Than Words 13
    Watch Out For The Double Standard 15
    The Dual Standard 16
    Identifying Specific Program Elements Can Be Tricky 17
    Starting Your Measurement Journey 22

Chapter 3 THE LANGUAGE OF MEASUREMENT: PRECISION ISSUES 23
    Does Terminology Make A Difference? 23
    Efficient vs. Productive vs. Effective 23
    Direct and Indirect 24
    Whole or Partial 25
    How Much Precision Is Really Required? 25
    Summary 30

Chapter 4 DESIGNING YOUR DIVERSITY MEASUREMENT SYSTEM FROM THE GROUND UP 31

Creating Measures Where None Exist .31
The Brainstorming Method 31
Nominal Group Technique 32
The Matrix Method 33
How to Create Measures Using the Matrix 44
Creating Formulas 40
Advanced Methods: the Family of Measures 43
Why a "Family" of Measures? 43
How to Construct a Family of Measures Objectives Matrix . . .46
Focus on Results 50

Chapter 5 ORGANIZING YOUR MEASURES: THE DIVERSITY 9-S FRAMEWORK 53

Applying a Strategic Link to the Organization 53
Shared Vision 57
Shared Values 57
Standards 58
Strategy 59
Structure 60
Systems 60
Skills 61
Style 62
Staff 62
Creating an Integrated Picture of the Diversity Effort 63

Chapter 6 DIVERSITY SHARED VISION, SHARED VALUES, AND STANDARDS: ESTABLISHING CORE SYSTEM MEASURES 69

Introduction 69
Measures to Support These Dimensions:
Diversity Vision, Values, and Standards 69
Shared Vision Measures 70
Shared Values Measures 70
Standards Measures 71
Applying Measures to Your Situation .71
Analyzing the Diversity Shared Vision Dimension 73
Shared Vision Measure-1 73
Shared Vision Measure-2 74

Contents

Shared Vision Measure-3 75
Shared Vision Measure-4 77
Shared Vision Measure-5 79
Analyzing the Diversity Shared Values Dimension 82
Shared Values Measure-1 82
Shared Values Measure-2 83
Shared Values Measure-3 84
Shared Values Measure-4 85
Analyzing the Diversity Standards Dimension 88

**Chapter 7 DIVERSITY STRATEGY, STRUCTURE, AND
SYSTEMS: ESTABLISHING TACTICAL, ORGANIZATIONAL
FORM, AND POLICY MEASURES** 93
Introduction 93
Measures That Support Diversity Strategy,
Structure, and Systems 94
Strategy Measures 94
Structure Measures 94
Systems Measures 95
Analyzing the Diversity Strategy Dimension 96
Strategy Measure-1 100
Strategy Measure-2 100
Strategy Measure-3 101
Analyzing the Diversity Structure Dimension 103
Structure Measure-1 103
Structure Measure-2 105
Structure Measure-3 106
Analyzing the Diversity Systems Dimension 108
Systems Measure-1 108
Systems Measure-2 109
Systems Measure-3 111
Systems Measure-4 114
Systems Measure-5 117
Systems Measure-6 120
Systems Measure-7 122
Policy Tracking Worksheet 123
Systems Measure-8 123
Age-Range Legend: 126

Chapter 8 DIVERSITY SKILLS: CREATING TRAINING EVALUATION MEASURES 129

Introduction 129

Evaluation 129

Types of Skill Development Measures .130

How Much Training Evaluation Do You Need? 131

Where Do You Begin? 132

Level 1: Participant Reactions 134

Participant Reactions: Rating Scale 137

Participant Reactions: Open-Ended 138

Level 2: Learning Outcomes 139

Self-Assessment of Learning 144

Diversity Pre- and Post-Course Self-Assessment 146

Diversity Role Play Checklist 147

Level 3: Transfer of Training 148

Participant Tool 151

Applying Diversity Training
On-the-Job: Participant Version 151

Manager's Tool 152

Satisfaction with Diversity
Training Course Effectiveness 152

Applying Diversity Training
On-the-Job: Manager's Version 154

Performance Checklist for
Diversity Training Transfer 155

Performance Change 156

Level 4: Organizational Results 157

Organizational Impact Evaluation 159

Level 5: Return on Training Investment 161

Chapter 9 DIVERSITY STAFF AND STYLE: DEVELOPING PERSONNEL AND CULTURAL MEASURES 167

Introduction 167

Measures Which Support These Dimensions:
Diversity Staff and Style 167

Staff Measures 168

Style Measures 168

Analyzing the Diversity Staff Dimension 169

Staff Measure-1 169

Staff Measure-2 173

Staffing Measure-3 174

Contents

Staffing Measure-4 175
Staffing Measure-5 177
Staffing Measure-6 179
Staffing Measure-7 181
Analyzing the Diversity Style Dimension 183
Style Measure-1 183
Style Measure-2 185
Style Measure-3 186
Style Measure-4 187
Five-by-Five Study Worksheet 190
Style Measure-5 191
Style Measure-6 192
Mentoring Analysis 194

Chapter 10 CONCLUSION:
THE STRATEGIC ADVANTAGE OF DIVERSITY 197
Contributing to the Bottom-Line 197

INDEX 201

REFERENCES 205

CHAPTER **1** Introduction

WHO SHOULD READ THIS BOOK

ARE YOU A DIVERSITY MANAGER ACCOUNTABLE for the implementation and direction of the organization's diversity efforts? A diversity consultant working with clients to help them transition to an inclusive, high-performance work environment? A diversity trainer responsible for training all levels of the organization to make everyone more aware and to build skills in managing a diverse work environment? An executive or manager in charge of a diverse work team accountable for organizational results? A top manager searching for a better understanding of issues concerning metrics related to diversity? If you are involved with designing and implementing a diverse work environment culture in any way, you will want to read this book.

Any of the above roles require you to share your expertise with others regarding possible approaches to make your work environment more inclusive for all employees. That is, building a culture that

If you are involved with designing and implementing a diverse work environment or culture in any way, you will want to read this book

In short, numbers drive the business

removes all barriers to individual and team performance and supports each employee in applying their absolute personal best efforts.

Business is and always has been a numbers or a bottom-line results game. With the advancements in information processing technology, today's executive has access to a range of data which is nearly infinite in its depth and breath. There is almost nothing that a computer can't process at incomprehensible speeds. Computers are churning numbers out on sales volume, accounts receivable and payable, production efficiency, market penetration, and hundreds of other subjects including projections for the future. The numbers tell management how much something costs, how many units are being produced and sold, how long the lead time is for delivery of parts or products. They are not only descriptive, they are also predictive. In short, they drive the business.

If diversity professionals want to be effective communicators in business around diversity issues, they must build rapport with their audiences

Periodically, businesses report on their progress by issuing press releases and filing required public reports with the government. Probably the most widely read report in private industry is the annual public relations product entitled the annual report. In government, one of the most widely read reports is the new budget projections. In both cases, the point is still the same...data in the form of numbers, process, impact, measurements, outcomes and/or results drive the lion's share of decision making processes in the organization.

There is no escaping numbers. Without them the line departments would have little idea of their performance. Also it would be impossible to report back to stakeholders and stockholders. This being the case, how does the diversity department or professional exist in this climate?

Some surveys of human resource professionals show that although they knew the number of employees in the company,

> "A majority of major corporation human resource professionals couldn't state the dollar volume of sales for their company, didn't know the profit level, and had little idea of the rate of return on corporate dollars invested."

> (Fitz-enz,1995)

These issues are all part of the daily lives of the line manager. The conclusion is somewhat obvious: if diversity professionals want to be effective communicators in business around diversity issues, they must build rapport with their audiences. The most direct way to do that is by recognizing their audience's values and use their language to communicate.

The metrics of diversity are still in their formative stages. However, as time goes on, it will become increasingly more important to have a firm grasp of the organization's effectiveness in utilizing the talents of all members of the work environment. This book will help you begin to meet these challenges head-on. In short, if you're charged with the task of evaluating diversity in any capacity, this book is for you so read on....

Tools in this book help locate increases in the value of your diversity efforts by providing a framework and help demonstrate diversity's organizational impact

WHEN AND HOW TO USE THIS BOOK

WHETHER YOU ARE PUTTING TOGETHER A DIVERSITY TRAINING program in a few weeks or implementing an ongoing diverse workforce culture change process, you want ready-to-use, effective measurement and evaluation tools. That's where Measuring Diversity Results can help. You can apply the tools, techniques and methods contained in this book before, during and throughout your diversity culture change process.

When tracking the success of your efforts, use the tools found throughout the book and particularly those in the chapters related to the "Diversity 9-S Framework" (which will be explained later). The tools in this book increase the value of your diversity efforts by providing a framework and demonstrating diversity's organizational impact. Use this book's tools to fully monitor the effectiveness of your diversity design and implementation efforts.

The following table may be helpful in guiding your use of the book. It is designed to help you quickly locate the measurement section of most interest to you. It is also helpful to read the remaining sections of the book to gain a more complete understanding of some of the issues surrounding measurement and diversity.

If you are interested in information covering...		Check out the information and/or tools in...
* You Can't Measure What We Do in Diversity Work...Can You??	⇨	Chapter Two
* The Language of Measurement: Precision Issues	⇨	Chapter Three
• Designing Your Diversity Measurement System From the Ground Up	⇨	Chapter Four
• Organizing Your Measures: The Diversity 9-S Framework	⇨	Chapter Five
• Diversity Shared Vision, Shared Values and Standards: Establishing Core System Measures	⇨	Chapter Six
• Diversity Strategy, Structure and Systems: Establishing Tactical, Organizational Form and Policy Measures	⇨	Chapter Seven
• Diversity Skills: Creating Training Evaluation Measures	⇨	Chapter Eight
• Diversity Staff and Style: Developing Personnel and Cultural Measures	⇨	Chapter Nine
• Conclusion: The Strategic Advantage of Diversity	⇨	Chapter Ten

The transition to diversity success in most organizations will be long and full of challenges. Similar to many organizational activities, supporters and doubters will look to measure the long-term benefits and value of diversity and where it falls amongst the organization's priorities.

Direction and control is virtually impossible without organized data and feedback. In addition, it is critical to understand the business in order to add value. Measuring Diversity Results will get you started by building on the fundamental language of business.

Direction and control is virtually impossible without organized data and feedback.

CHAPTER 2 You Can't Measure What We Do In Diversity Work...Can You??

IT'S ALL SUBJECTIVE

IF YOU WERE TO ANALYZE MANY ORGANIZATIONAL EFFORTS to transition to a diverse work environment, a strange paradox would emerge: While a persuasive case can be made for the economic benefits of managing and leveraging diversity, this critical outcome is rarely emphasized in most strategic business initiatives.

In fact, in many organizations it appears that the business case for diversity is deliberately left out of the discussion. It almost seems counter-intuitive that this potentially powerful argument is omitted so often in organizations that have service, growth, profitability, and customer-focused marketing strategies at the top of their list of goals and objectives.

> It appears that the business case for diversity is deliberately left out of the discussion

There seems to be a myth operating within business and governmental communities which suggest that the outcomes or results created by a diversity implementation process defies measurement or can only be measured in the long-term. In a sense, its presented with the fundamental belief that creating an effective diverse, inclusive work environment is something of a complex and mysterious art form. Allegedly, the real value of diversity work can only be judged by those who perform it, those who are truly committed to its purpose or value it as important, etc. Even then, the assessment of the results is saddled with subjectivity.

> The lack of measurement practices for diversity sets managing and leveraging diversity apart from the rest of the organization.

Some diversity specialists perceive that there is an inherent conflict between what is good for business and what is good for people. Some others believe, like truth, that the real reward is in the work itself. The words often used to describe the results include terms such as working better, appreciating differences, understanding each other better, less conflict, getting along, working as a team, and other similar non-measurement specific words. While these are admirable aims in themselves they are not enough. Especially when organizations are looking for strategies to deal with increased competition, options for reducing cost, adding value, adding dollars and increasing productivity to affect the bottom-line.

These notions seem to imply that quantifiable and quality-based measures cannot be applied to the diversity implementation process or a diverse work culture. Some people even believe that diversity is not a business focused activity, simply another form of affirmative action regulatory compliance, even though demographics, which are irrefutable, have been set in motion which makes diversity not only a business and customer issue, but a global competitive issue!

Whether the subjective position is valid or not is a key question to be sure. However, just the fact that it exists and that some diversity professionals and other business people support it creates major problems. It sets managing and leveraging diversity apart from the rest of the organization. While peers in other organizational areas are focusing on metrics which reflect their contribution such as sales, reduced costs, profits, income and expenses, etc., those implementing the diversity process may limit its contribution to increased awareness, improved feelings and increased satisfaction among groups. It is a real missed opportunity.

Some line managers quickly make judgments about diversity being a "soft," non-business oriented endeavor which contributes little to bottom line performance. In addition, these managers may also assume that those involved in diversity neither understand or are interested in measuring diversity's contribution to the organization. As a result, diversity is not taken seriously, fewer managers support it in actual practice i.e., sending their workforce to be trained, structuring their workforce to leverage its richness through teaming, implementing strategic human resource advantages to penetrate key ethnic customer markets, etc. We know from current organizational practice that diversity initiatives experience less follow-through than other business initiatives. Many diversity managers resent this second-hand treatment, yet it is inevitable given the lack of a common connection and language which is fundamental to business.

> Many diversity managers resent this second-hand treatment, yet it is inevitable given the lack of a common connection and language which is critical to business.

REASONS WHY NOT

THERE ARE A NUMBER OF REASONS WHY THERE IS A LACK of quantification in diversity. Probably the most prevalent is that diversity professionals simply do not know how to objectively measure diversity activities.

Statistical courses are not always a part of many human resource development curricula.

The focus on diverse workforce management and development is still relatively new. In addition, there are many routes into diversity and the process of diverse workforce development. Few, if any, offer training in quantitative methods. Many diversity professionals are still trying to understand all of the implications of diverse workforce trends in the national and global arena. Since there are few predecessors, it is not surprising that many diversity professionals still rely on subjective measures.

Some practitioners in the diversity field have human resources backgrounds and have had the opportunity to study human resource development in college. Unfortunately, statistical courses are not always a part of many human resource development curricula. Even when they are, they tend to be either financial or behavioral science methods. Statistical procedures have seldom been adapted to the creation of input-output ratios for measuring diversity processes or a human resources function's results. The reason for this is fairly simple: many of the academic processes have never really been applied to the problem. There are some schools and individuals who have developed a measures such as Dr. Taylor Cox Jr., at the University of Michigan in his book: *Cultural Diversity In Organizations: Theory, Research & Practice*, or Lawrence M. Baytos, who co-published a book with the Society for Human Resources Management entitled: *Designing & Implementing*

Successful Diversity Programs in which he devotes a chapter on the subject of measuring benefits and maintaining momentum. I'm certain there are others, perhaps many corporate examples as well which we know little about, nonetheless, diversity practitioners have little to choose from until more people chronicle their efforts in a form that makes the tools more accessible. In addition, there are virtually no offering in the public seminar market devoted to this subject in detail. All-in-all, for someone who wants to start a measurement system in their organizations for the change to a more inclusive, diverse workforce there is very little help available.

The second reason behind the subjectivity myth is the values conflict. Some believe that objective measurement is simply inappropriate for diversity work. In their eyes, diversity work is a function devoted to stimulating and supporting human development, and they see no reason to evaluate outcomes in other than humanitarian terms. This one-sided approach is prevalent in many occupations. Some managers believe the sole mission of training is to transfer technical information about work from one person's brain into the brains of the workers. This is the technical competency model of human development. They see no real responsibility to teach workers to think, evaluate, or form values. Some architects believe their job is to create a container within which some kind of activity can be efficiently carried out. They overlook the fact that human beings interact with the space and can be depressed or stimulated by it. These perspectives ignore the holistic philosophies of systemic organizational views.

For those whose value system conflicts with the notion of measuring diversity, there is little hope for change...unless they experience a "significant emotional event" like losing their diversity job, funding, and/or support.

For those whose value system conflicts with the notion of measuring diversity, there is little hope for change...unless they experience a "significant emotional event" like losing their diversity job, funding, and/or support because it is thought that very little value is derived from their diversity work. Even then some people still may not "get it." Until they expand their outlook to include supporting the strategic purpose of the organization, there will be the perception that management should just see this as "a good thing" or the "right thing" to do.

What if you're making terrific progress and don't know it?

Another very common reason why diversity departments or diversity activities are not measured is that some diversity professionals fear measurement. Perhaps it is born out of a fear of knowing. However, if you don't know, you can almost guarantee that nothing will ever improve. But what if you're making terrific progress and don't know it? What if several areas were doing a great job in leveraging the diverse talents of their work groups and are beginning to slip back into old, less effective habits? Key opportunities for adjustment and reinforcement would be missed. The implications of this can be mind-boggling. This bring us to the fourth and last reason for the subjectivity myth.

Some members of top management have bought the myth of subjectivity... but not for long!

Some members of top management have bought the myth of subjectivity...but not for long! Perhaps because for a long time, there has been little interest in human resources issues. The early captains of industry simply never asked the question. As time progressed, the tradition of nonmeasureability went unchallenged. Few CEOs have taken more than a cursory tour in the human resources department during their careers. It was often just a quick stop along the way to the executive suite. Just about the time they were beginning to sink their teeth into what could be accomplished and what may need to be changed, they were off to another "developmental assignment." Many of these budding executives, knowing the assignment would be a brief 12–18 months, looked for quick projects with a lot of visibility. Very few embarked upon major, fundamental projects which would touch all facets of the human resources department. However, today this is changing.

ACTIONS SPEAK LOUDER THAN WORDS

RIGHT SIZING, DOWNSIZING, REENGINEERING, reorganizations and other buzzwords depict widespread department cuts, sizable employee layoffs, and significant budget reductions without regards to the impact on workforce diversity.

The goal of these efforts? To eliminate functions that do not add value to the bottom line. Senior executives are examining all areas of the organization to determine contribution levels and alignment with strategic and competitive goals of the organization. If organizational departments or efforts cannot demonstrate levels of contribution, they are considered suspect.

In a recent article in the Philadelphia Inquirer, this trend was confirmed with the headline: "As the year ends, companies step up the pace of layoffs:"

> It happens whenever new budgets are approved. But this year has brought more and bigger cuts. The list reads like a roster of blue-chip corporations: AT&T, IBM, 3M, Sprint, Fruit of the Loom, Bell South, and more. During the past

Senior executives are examining all areas of the organization to determine contribution levels and alignment with strategic and competitive goals of the organization.

More and more,
performance
measures are being
used to evaluate the
effectiveness of
every aspect of an
organization;
diversity is no
exception.

month, companies at the heart of corporate America have announced plans to reduce their workforces—in many cases, by the thousands...AT&T Corp. dropped a blockbuster Wednesday with word it was offering severance packages to almost 78,000 managers to trim its payroll by a yet-to-be-disclosed number. Sprint announced 1,600 cuts the same day. Minnesota Mining & Manufacturing Co. (3M) said Tuesday it was cutting 5,000 positions in a restructuring.... The reductions this fall come as companies struggle to increase profits in a slow growth economic climate. Some cutbacks are merger-related. Others are pure cost-cutting. For many companies, though, the job reductions are merely steps in an ongoing process.... Stephen S. Roach, chief economist at Morgan Stanley & Co., the Wall Street investment firm, says that by year-end the number of layoffs reported since March 1991, when the recovery from the 1990 recession began, will be 2.5 Million. "That's a carnage without precedent," he said.

Source: The Philadelphia Inquirer, November 18, 1995, p. D1

So, how does your organization's diversity efforts measure up? Does diversity in your organization bring value to the bottom line or strategic outcomes, or is it perceived as a luxury well suited for the ax? You have an opportunity to be a proactive force (rather than a reactive protector) in communicating the success and value of your diversity efforts. You can have positive, open discussions regarding the effects of the organization's diversity efforts on its financial, strategic, human capital development, and competitive goals. More and more, performance measures are being used to evaluate the effectiveness of every aspect of an organization; diversity is no exception.

WATCH OUT FOR THE DOUBLE STANDARD

THE PRECEDING DISCUSSION SHOULD NOT SUGGEST THAT measurement is the panacea "cure-all" to diversity's acceptance into the corporate landscape. Measurement applied to diversity or any other human resource area is fraught with complexity among a cluttered canvass of contributors who claim to contribute to bottom-line outcomes of the organization. Remember, diversity activities are not conducted in a vacuum.

For organizations that are simultaneously going through activities such as terminating employees, major reorganizations and mergers, reengineering, etc., how do you separate the specific effects of the diversity programs with any degree of accuracy? It should be understood from the outset that the attribution of specific causes and effects will not be easy (Baytos, 1995).

> It should be understood from the outset that the attribution of specific causes and effects will not be easy.

As mentioned earlier, measuring diversity results has generated a wide range of views concerning what should be done. In many cases, the views are polar opposites. Efforts range from subcommittees charged with the task of generating metrics to those who are content with the notion that diversity supports the overall vision and strategy, and are willing to settle for subjective assessments of the value of the programs, much as they would do for management development programs or communications activities.

It's no surprise that measuring diversity results is beginning to surface more in corporate discussions, given the context of recent business trends and pressures for improved performance. But before we can delve into the subject of what and how to measure, we must discuss the potential measurement pitfalls you can and should avoid.

THE DUAL STANDARD

"WHILE I DON'T QUESTION THE SINCERITY OF THE INTEREST in identifying the value of diversity interventions, I sometimes wonder if companies are attempting to apply a tougher standard of evaluation for diversity processes than they do for other ongoing activities." (Baytos, 1995) I also agree this notion is an important consideration. There are numerous organizational activities that have little or no measurement support to justify their existence, yet they continue to be upheld vigorously by top management.

> The real question is should diversity activities be held to a much tougher standard than other company programs?

For example, those who might be demanding some specific proofs for diversity programming, at the same time will be moving ahead on the following activities. A meeting costing $500,000 held for key managers and their significant others for "sharing of the strategic plan and the chairman's vision, etc. The meeting is held at a posh resort during the work week, and much of the time is spent on the golf course, cocktail parties and tennis courts. The activity is felt to be essential to "morale, commitment, communications" and so on, but there is no attempt to measure the specific impact of the meeting.

Additions are made to the company jet fleet, and company limo service is expanded to enhance "executive productivity," without indicating how that productivity will specifically benefit shareholders, over and above the costs of the services.

(Baytos, 1995)

The real question is should diversity activities (that potentially benefit so many employees as well as delivering business benefits to the organization) be held to a much tougher standard than other company programs? And will the duality of this application of measurement standards in the workplace infer to employees an underlying bias or lack of commitment to diversity as the reason? It certainly raises the question!

IDENTIFYING SPECIFIC PROGRAM ELEMENTS CAN BE TRICKY

BROAD-BASED DIVERSITY INITIATIVES WILL PROCEED along several lines at the same time if they are systemic. All of these activities such as child-care services, flexi-time, flexi-place strategies, parental leave options, and others could be in action simultaneously. Let's suppose that at the end of a two year period, management notes a 45 percent decrease in turnover among female managers. The impact of this decrease is an identifiable value to the organization in lower recruiting and training costs. However, which of the above programs caused the improvement during that period?

The reality is you may never know. But this scenario should not diminish the need or quest to locate effective measures. There are several measures that can and should be a part of the diversity toolkit for performance feedback. A sample list is shown from Baytos in the following tables:

Activity Focus	Measurement	Potential Profit Impact
Affirmative Action Hiring & Retention	1. Numbers of females and minorities hired versus • previous years actual • percentage in the applicant flow • percentages of area availability as determined by EEOC data	Good results cut risk of costly compliance sanctions

Activity Focus	Measurement	Potential Profit Impact
	2. Turnover of females and minorities versus • % for white males • previous year's trend line • external benchmark	Lower turnover can • reduce costs of recruiting replacements • reduce training costs • reduce expenses and lost revenues due to inexperience of new employees in jobs
	3. Percentage of mothers who return from maternity leave.	Same as above
Upward Mobility of target groups	Number of females and minorities in key management positions and on back-up slates.	Reduced expenses for advertising, search and other employment costs to fill openings
Climate for Diversity	% of favorable responses to survey questions as compared with • previous survey • division within the company • external benchmarks	Early warning on developing issues can be used to avert high turnover, EEO charges, which in turn reduces costs (see above and below)
EEO Complaints	Number of AA/EEO related complaints per 1,000 employees as compared with • previous years • other parts of the company • community or industry benchmark	Reduced complaints lower cost of staff to investigate and defend company, and provide financial settlements
EEO Legal Action	Cost of settlement of EEO charges (see above)	Reduced legal and court costs, reduced costs of settling cases.

Activity Focus	Measurement	Potential Profit Impact
Community Outreach	Amount of business done with minority/female-owned organizations.	May not have direct dollar benefit for purchaser
Program Flexibility	% of employees at various levels, age/race/gender utilizing options in flexible compensation and benefit programs.	Satisfaction provided through more flexible use of current programs may forestall the need for costly enhancements, or make it possible to reduce other benefits with limited negative impact on employees
	Number of employees using flexible hours, job sharing, telecommute	Same as above plus reduced turnover costs and reduced costs associated with unplanned absenteeism
Compensation Equity Analysis	Wage and salary adjustments in excess of guideline increases	Correction of pay inequities adds to expense, but may reduce future costs of excessive turnover and defense of EEO charges and suits
Training & Development	Increased numbers of females, minorities using development programs	Increased satisfaction reduces turnover and its associated costs and builds needed competencies within the organization
Productivity	Performance of homogeneous work groups versus diverse work teams • Output quantity • Quality • Time to complete	Greater output reduces cost per unit, increasing profits. Greater creativity produces new products, ideas.

Activity Focus	Measurement	Potential Profit Impact
Diversity Related Training, *e.g.*, sexual harassment	Number of complaints, dollar value of settlements	Reduced legal fees and settlement costs increase profits
Marketing to Diverse Consumers	Sales and market share before and after programs generated by diverse marketing team	Sales dollar and profits from those sales

As time goes on, more and more information demonstrating benefits will become available. Baytos also highlights examples of information now in the public domain which is summarized in the following table:

Source/Organization	Program Type	Benefit Claimed
Business Week, American Airlines	"Supertrack" for female managers to provide more rapid advancement.	Increased women in upper levels from 12% to 21% in a five year period
Chicago Tribune Allstate Insurance	Work and family initiatives (broad)	The program saves money. It costs us $30-60,000 to train employees. Work and family programs help keep turnover low
OAG	On-site day care center	Post maternity turnover reduced from 44% to 22%
Wall Street Journal, Corning	Training in gender awareness ("Women as Colleagues")	Used to spend $4 Million per year recruiting and training women. Since the diversity training started the dropout rate and expense has been cut in half

Source/Organization	Program Type	Benefit Claimed
HR Magazine, Nynex	Mentoring circles for females and minorities	• Increase gender awareness by male mentors • Defuse potential serious sexual harassment situations • Provide visibility for upper level positions • Builds support system to improve productivity on the job
Wall Street Journal, Conference Board Survey	Flexible work programs-employer rationale *e.g.*, Du Pont, Avon, Knight Ridder News, IBM	• Recruiting advantage • Increase productivity • Reduce turnover
Wall Street Journal	Understanding differences training	Improved understanding and reduced friction in working with non-U.S. employees
Avon	Employee advocacy groups	Provide solidarity and career help for members, tackle subconscious
Harvard Business Review, Digital	Training of thousands of employees in valuing or understanding differences	Help transform legal and social pressure into the competitive advantage of a more effective work force.
Wall Street Journal, Northern States Power, Helene Curtis, Household International	Mentoring & Networking programs	• Doubled the number of women officers/managers • Turnover of new mothers reduced from 31% to 7% • Cut new mother turnover from 40% to 25%

STARTING YOUR MEASUREMENT JOURNEY

This book will help you begin the journey of measuring your diversity results. It is by no means all inclusive, yet it can provide a starting point. You can use these measurements to improve diversity efforts that fall short and identify winning approaches and processes that work to transform the organization's culture!

You will be able to show how really fruitful your efforts are...and have been. As a diversity professional, it is both a necessity and a responsibility to demonstrate the value of current workforce diversity efforts and to show that diversity does have outcomes and payoffs which relate to bottom line performance and strategic objectives.

As a diversity professional, it is both a necessity and a responsibility to demonstrate the value of current workforce diversity effort.

Sound challenging? Perhaps, but using a few practical tools can begin to pave the way toward success! This book will help you measure the value of your workforce diversity efforts, making the process less complicated and more rewarding. In general, you will be able to:

- *Check that you have planned for success,*

- *Actually measure your efforts, and*

- *Communicate your findings.*

The tools in this book help you increase the value of your workforce diversity efforts by providing focus and demonstrating organizational impact. If full diverse workforce utilization is to be a reality in our lifetime, we must use every tool or resource available to fully monitor and communicate the effectiveness of this effort.

CHAPTER 3 The Language of Measurement: Precision Issues

DOES TERMINOLOGY MAKE A DIFFERENCE?

YES! TO MEASURE DIVERSITY RESULTS EFFECTIVE-LY, it is helpful to become familiar with basic terms and to discuss fundamental issues. The focus of this effort is to clarify key issues in measurement and to avoid semantic debates. Words we use to describe observable outcomes in diversity are, by their very nature, only symbols. People sometimes give them meaning in a rather haphazard fashion. This practice is particularly true in the case of the words efficient, productive, and effective. In everyday conversation, these terms often are used interchangeably. Though the dictionary definitions are similar, the terms connote slightly different outcomes.

EFFICIENT VS. PRODUCTIVE VS. EFFECTIVE

PRODUCTIVE IS DEFINED AS "PRODUCING READILY or abundantly." Synonyms for productive are profitable, fertile, and fruitful. The definition of efficient is "competent or adequate in performance

> Words we use to describe observable outcomes in diversity are, by their very nature, only symbols. People sometimes give them meaning in a rather haphazard fashion.

or operation." The meaning is similar to productive but implies something less potent. Capable and causative are synonyms for efficient. So, while both productive and efficient are positive terms, productive implies something beyond merely being competent. The third word, effective, takes the notion of productivity and adds the notions of expectation and desirability. Management Scientist Peter Drucker refers to it as "doing the right thing." Another definition of effectiveness is, "having the desired effect or producing the expected result."

With this as a foundation, we can use efficient to mean simply an acceptable level of performance. Productive means efficiency directed at activities that have real value. An example might be a case where someone performs a task quickly and neatly. However, the task adds nothing to the output of the diversity effort and cannot be described as productive because it does not serve the purpose of valuing and/or managing diversity.

DIRECT AND INDIRECT

TWO OTHER WORDS, DIRECT AND INDIRECT, WILL BE USED to describe different types of measurements. A direct measure is one that refers to cost. It could be the cost of a diversity hiring effort or the cost of a diversity training program. An indirect measure does not deal with cost. It could be a measure of time, quantity, or quality. In many cases indirect measures can be converted to direct measures through the introduction of a simple conversion variable.

An example: the conversion of the indirect measure of the time needed to interview, as part of a diversity staffing effort, into the direct measure of the cost of interviewing. If we know that on average interviewers need one and one-half hours to interview a potential candidate for the workforce, and if we know the hourly pay rate of the interviewers, it is a simple matter to multiply that pay rate by one and one-half to obtain the cost of the interview. This is a simplistic example. Obviously, other costs are involved in an interview. However, depending on how precise you want to be, you can add in overhead and benefit costs, or any other cost items that seem appropriate, to obtain the total cost of the interview. The point is this: Indirect performance data can be valuable to development of a direct measure.

WHOLE OR PARTIAL

A SUBSET OF BOTH DIRECT AND INDIRECT MEASURES is the difference between whole and partial measures. Whole measures describe the total issue. For example, the cost per hire, which includes every expense item, is a whole measure. However, if you are only calculating the cost per hire using a particular diversity recruiting source, you are working toward creating a partial measure of the total diversity hiring costs. In the case of this partial measurement, all other costs are givens, and you would want only to know the cost per hire for this particular diversity recruiting source.

Whole measures are informative on a broad basis. If you want to learn where you are spending most of your time or money, you will dissect the whole measure into two or more categories or parts. By breaking down total costs by source, department, job level, race, sex, occupation, and other categories, you can find out where the problems lie or where the opportunities for improvement are.

HOW MUCH PRECISION IS REALLY REQUIRED?

ANY TIME THE SUBJECT OF MEASURING HUMAN RESOURCES or diversity work comes up, issues of accuracy and precision invariably arise. It has been argued that to measure diversity activities convincingly or with any high degree of confidence is difficult. Diversity measures based on "report cards" don't allow for competing hypotheses in assertions such as "managing diversity leads to increased profitability." (Some would argue that other efforts could just as easily have caused the profitability to increase). Another contention is that there is lack of control over thousands of factors that influence a large organization's profitability. That is, lack of control over factors like inflation, labor market conditions, and cost of money can make it virtually impossible to effectively measure diversity with accuracy.

In general, this argument is correct, though similar conditions prevail throughout the organization. Everyone knows certain factors are not controllable. The marketing department does not have control over the product or the customer; the finance department does not control the cost of money. Yet both departments are able to evaluate much of their work quantitatively. If we are willing, we might admit that there are more issues out of control than in the control of any organization. The task of management is to reduce the uncontrollable variables and to instill as much order as possible.

Management does not require accuracy at the .05 level of statistical significance. In research, precision is critical, obviously. In pharmaceuticals or medicine, extreme care must be taken with procedures and measurement. Results are often required to be statistically valid beyond the .001 level. That kind of measurement with a capital "M" is not required in operational measurement. We are operating not in a laboratory, but in the field, with all the problems inherent in field research and experimentation. Accuracy is necessary, but precision is naturally limited by internal and external conditions. Though we can't control the variables in the environment completely, we can still come up with usable numbers.

It is not necessary to introduce heavy statistics to persuade management and employees of the need for progress and accountability in diversity culture change initiatives and to highlight their impact on profitability. This does not suggest that mental models approaches and control group processes (explained later) should be avoided. It suggests only that the optimum array of diversity measures should include a blend of data and levels of measurement. In many business situations, activity- and process-based (report card) diversity measures can play a vital role in the organization's leadership agenda.

Report card measures of diversity are like snapshots of the past. They can provide a historical reference to accomplishments or serve as milestones along the path to producing outcomes. Examples: the number of diversity training sessions completed, cost per diversity trainee-hour, and turnover by performance level by gender by length of service. These measures provide opportunities for personal feedback regarding compliance and measuring accountability for implementing new diverse workforce change or improvement activities and processes. These report card measures are a key part of a value chain for implementing change in an organization.

This value chain is comprised of four basic components:

Generally speaking, all processes are begun for the purpose of producing value. Any other purpose would be wasteful. One of our objectives should be to develop more effective ways to measure and evaluate changes in the organization's diversity improvement activities/processes, outcomes, impact, and resulting value.

Some typical value chain examples:

Activity/Process	Outcome	Impact	Value-Added
• Increase Diverse Talent Recruitment Sources	• Lower Agency Rates	• Lower Hiring Costs	Reduced Operating Expense
• Improve Diverse Work Team Problem-Solving Processes	• Reduced Time to Solve	• Increase in Reason Given in Survey for Long Service by Diverse Member	• Retention Savings as Compared to Rolling Average of Previous Years
• Install Succession Planning for Diverse Workforce	• Fewer Emergency Minority Hires	• Less Recruitment Expense	• Lower Operating Expense

For every use of resources to improve an organization using a diversity activity/process, there should be an improvement in result. We call the result an outcome. The difference between this outcome and the previous outcomes before the diversity process improvement was implemented is the impact. The dollar improvement represented by the impact is the value added. An example is to change the sourcing methods used to hire diverse workforce talent (activities/process), which shortens the time to fill jobs (outcome).

Time-to-Fill Formula: TF = RR - OD where:

TF = Time to have an offer accepted

RR = Date the requisition is received (*e.g.*, January 4)

OD = Date the offer is accepted (*e.g.*, February 20)

EXAMPLE

TF = January 4 - February 20

= 47 days

As jobs are filled faster (see impact 1), there is less need to use temporary or contract workers (see impact 2). The cost avoidance can be calculated and a dollar savings computed (see value added 1). If, through the diversity department's effort to change sourcing methods, jobs are filled faster, not only does the organization reduce operating expense, but the cost of the human resource product is lowered and moved to market faster (see value added 2). Lower human resource (product) acquisition cost and shorter human resource asset delivery time to the organization can create a competitive advantage (see value added 3), especially in light of less successful competitors (based upon benchmarking analysis comparisons).

Thus, report card measures of diversity activities and/or processes are vital in order to gain feedback on staff accountability for generating solutions to address such key business issues as inadequate diverse talent acquisition. Without these activities or processes, we could not produce the accompanying outcomes, impacts and results. Even if these activities or processes produced poor results, the diversity department can gain by knowing what else doesn't work and then shift its efforts to more productive outcomes.

Performance measurement of the type reflected in calculations such as the "Time to Fill" measure illustrated earlier, can be handled with basic arithmetic functions.

Though measures such as these are often thought to be too simplistic to be effective, a story by Jac Fitz-enz is appropriate:

> "On one occasion a professor from a midwestern university complained that my method for measuring human resources, although effective, was too simplistic. My reply was, 'If you think these formulas are too simple a way to express the conditions they observe, how would you evaluate $E = mc^2$?' He replied, 'I don't know anything about chemistry'."

> Jac Fitz-enz, "How to Measure Human Resources Management," Saratoga Institute, 1995

For the most part, any object, issue, act, process, or activity that can be described by observable variables is subject to measurement. The phenomenon can be evaluated in terms of cost, time, quantity, or quality. The central issue in applying measurement to the diversity culture change process is this: to decide what is worth measuring and to agree on the measure as a fair representation of progress and accountability (given field limitations). Often, management will accept progress over perfection.

SUMMARY

SUCCESS IS ACHIEVED THROUGH PERFORMANCE. Performance is more than activity. Each activity must be turned toward adding value. Most of those values must be measurable. In order to measure, it is vital to learn how to use simple arithmetic data to illustrate the value of the workforce diversity effort.

The primary language of business is numbers, not feelings. Some people are afraid of numbers. They will use every excuse they can find to avoid having to deal numerically. People often fear the data will be used to hurt them. The irony is that numbers can be used very effectively to demonstrate how well the diversity effort is doing. Isn't it worth knowing before someone else tells you how well your diversity effort is doing with their numbers?

Though accuracy is imperative, precision is not. A business enterprise operates in an uncontrollable environment. Even salespeople cannot prove that it was their sales capabilities alone that won an order. Statistical proof is not the point. Management often just wants to know: Are we moving in the right direction? Are the workforce diversity efforts we have in place helping us to meet key strategic workforce and bottom-line organizational objectives? Diversity professionals know it's important to provide the answers.

CHAPTER 4 Designing Your Diversity Measurement System From the Ground Up

CREATING MEASURES WHERE NONE EXIST

HALF THE BATTLE OF CREATING DIVERSITY MEASURES where none exists is simply a matter of having an analytical process that works and a proven framework that provides a comprehensive look at what to measure. Any one of the following four methods can be used to find measurable events and each method is equally valid. The four are:

☐ The Brainstorming Method

☐ The Nominal Group Technique

☐ The Matrix Method

☐ The Family of Measures Method

Some are more complex than others, but all are easy to understand and execute.

> Any one of four methods can be used to find measurable events. Each method is equally valid.

THE BRAINSTORMING METHOD

THE FIRST AND MOST COMMON WAY OF DEVELOPING A LIST of just about anything is the tried and proven brainstorming method. Most everyone is familiar with this approach. A group of people is given a question or a problem to solve. This is the question: "Among all the activities occurring within our diversity effort or initiatives, what can we quantitatively measure?" The participants are given time to deliberate and then are asked for their answers. All suggestions are taken and recorded without any judgments being rendered until all the ideas have been exhausted. It is normal to list these on a chart pad, board, or computer so that everyone can see and review them.

Often the sight of one measure triggers the idea of another. After all the ideas are on display, the group goes back through the list and selects those they agree are worth working on. People are more likely to be motivated by a measure they had some part in selecting. This method is relatively quick, and it gives everyone a chance to contribute. However, it usually does not produce as many measures as the other methods.

Nominal Group Technique

A SECOND, LESS COMMON, BUT MORE POWERFUL, APPROACH is the nominal group technique (NGT). This method is similar to brainstorming in some respects. They both start with the same question and in both cases the participants have time to deliberate.

In NGT the participants generate their ideas in writing. Then, in round-robin fashion each member of the group offers one idea in a short phrase, which is recorded on a flip chart, board, or in a computer. After all ideas are recorded, each is checked with the group for clarification and evaluation. The final step is individual voting on the items by priority, with the group decision being mathematically derived through rank-ordering or rating. The nominal group technique is a highly developed form of brainstorming. Research has shown that if the task is idea generation, NGT produces more and better quality ideas than the standard brainstorming session.

THE MATRIX METHOD

THE THIRD METHOD OF MEASURES GENERATION IS THE MATRIX. Though the first two measurement generation approaches work well, at some point you may find yourself simply recycling through about 15 to 20 measures. At that point, an alternate approach will be needed.

Someone once said, "You can't find new ways of doing things by looking at them harder in the old way." Nothing could be closer to this truth than in measurement. Recycling through the same old measures does not give you a better understanding of what's happening in your diversity efforts. It is often helpful to think of creating measures based upon what is happening in the organization to develop a full sense of what's going on and how well diversity initiatives are being implemented.

With this notion in mind, you can radically change your approach. Instead of looking for specific things to measure, the measurement system can be based upon methods to more fully understand what is going on in the organization and how diversity initiatives can support the organization's strategic objectives.

Starting there, you can began to describe your work environment variable by variable. Taking one function at a time, you ask, "If we walk into Department "X" tomorrow, what will we see in the way of activities, behavior, and/or results that are directly or indirectly related to our diversity initiatives?" "How are these efforts linked to the strategic goals and objectives of the organization?" You can begin by listing every variable, process, or thing observed. Next, you place each thing, variable or process on a matrix and cross-match every variable. The number of measurable activities explodes.

The objective is to find what in statistics are known as dependent variables. In this case, a dependent variable not only is an activity subject to quantifiable measurement but whose value or cost can be increased or decreased through the manipulation of other factors known as independent variables.

For example, if we want to assess the benefit versus the cost of diversity training, we could start measuring the cost per trainee hour (CTH) of our instruction as compared to key diversity climate and culture survey statistics. CTH is the dependent variable. In order to calculate that value, we need to know all cost items of the diversity training. This might include material expense, instructor salary, participants' salaries, travel expense, and room and refreshment cost. We also need to know how many people were trained and how many hours each was trained. These items are independent variables. By changing any of the independent variables we affect the dependent variable. We will see an example of this later in the book.

To summarize: The matrix measurement development method is a two- step process. First, we generate a list of dependent variables to measure. Then, for each dependent variable. we decide which independent variables go into the calculation. With them, you can construct a formula that becomes part of your system of measures. In many trials I have always found that the matrix method is superior to brainstorming or a nominal group technique for generating a larger number of measures whose quality is at least equal to those resulting from other approaches.

How to Create Measures Using the Matrix

THE EASIEST WAY TO DESCRIBE THE MATRIX METHOD is by example. Let us say that we want to generate a large list of measures to track diversity in staffing. The first question: "If you walk into the staffing department, what do you see?" You see people: the staffing manager, supervisors, recruiters, clerks, applicants, new hires, and client managers (those looking to fill jobs in their group or department). You see things: applications and resumes, requisitions, furniture and equipment, office spaces, bills for ads and agency fees, travel vouchers, referral bonus checks, and job postings. You see processes going on: interviews, application screening, telephone calls, counseling, selection and rejection, record processing, and filing.

All of these variables are subject to at least one of the four dimensions of measurement. Each can be analyzed according to its cost, the time it takes to do it, its quantity or volume or frequency of occurrence, or its quality. At this stage it is not important to know which of these attributes applies. All you want to do here is to fully describe the environment of the staffing department and the activities related to the diversity staffing initiative. Once you have a full description, you probably will be amazed at the size of the list. There should be at least two or three dozen variables. If you are meticulous in your observations, you may find many more than that. You may think that the list is too large, but don't feel overwhelmed. The list can be reduced without loss of value.

Go back over the list and decide if there are variables you are not interested in measuring or do not directly relate to your diversity staffing initiatives. You undoubtedly will find items that may be combined with others into a larger classification or are not important to look at now. An example of the first type: furniture and equipment, office spaces, heat, and light. These are normally grouped into an account titled overhead. By substituting overhead for a half-dozen other variables, you not only shorten the list but also have a variable with meaning. Each of the specific simple variables deals with an issue which, in and of itself, probably does not have much importance. However, when combined with the others to make an overhead category, the variable becomes complex and may be worth looking at.

In the second type of exclusion, some items simply have no value. You may decide that the number or duration of telephone calls is not an interesting measure. You could decide to include the telephone bill in general overhead, or you might decide to ignore it except within the total department budget or expenditure. Filing is another example of a variable with little value. If you ask yourself what is really important about the staffing function and diversity-related initiatives, the key variables become apparent. Once you have reduced the list to a manageable number, you are ready for the next step.

The figure shown below is a sample of the matrix form you can use to lay out your variables.

DIVERSITY MEASUREMENT MATRIX							
	Cost	Recruiter	Diversity Applicant Source	Diversity Hires	Diversity Requisition	Time	Etc.
Cost							
Recruiter							
Diversity Applicant Source							
Diversity Hires							
Diversity Requisition							
Time							
Etc.							

Referring to your final list of useful variables, begin to place them on the grid. Starting at the top left corner, put one variable on each line vertically down the left side. Start with cost, then recruiter, and proceed in any order you want thereafter. Do not worry that these variables are all opposite shaded spaces on the grid. Since you will probably have a list that exceeds 20 variables, I suggest that you do this on a couple of chart-pad sheets taped together. The grid should be large enough to place a line both vertically and horizontally for each variable on your final list.

When you have finished going down the grid, turn your attention to the spaces across the top. Again, beginning at the top left corner of the grid, write in one variable per line going left to right across the top of the grid. ***These must be in the same order as the one you used vertically***. For example, you started your vertical list with cost and recruiter and let's say you followed with diversity applicant source, diversity hires, diversity requisition, time, etc. Your horizontal list must also start with cost and recruiter and follow the same sequence from left to right across the top of the grid. The end product should be a grid that has the same list of variables running down the side as it does across the top. You will then have created a matrix of useful variables.

The next procedure is to begin to match a vertical variable with a horizontal variable line by line. The grid has 49 cells or squares. Each cell is a combination of two variables: one from the list on the side and one from the list on the top. The first thing you would notice, if none of the cells were shaded, is that the top left corner cell is a combination of the same variable from the top and from the side. This is really not a combination, is it? It is redundant. If we were to create a dependent variable called cost per cost, it would be nonsense. Hence, redundant cells are useless. But if you go to the next line down and across, you find that recruiter and recruiter fill the second cell down and the second cell in to create another redundancy. Following that pattern you see that there is a line of redundant cells running from the top left corner to the bottom right corner. All of them are useless and, therefore, have been shaded.

But, what about all the other cells to the left? They are not redundant, but they are duplicates of cells to the right. To test them, select two variables, such as diversity hires (across) and time (down). They are the fourth and sixth variables, respectively, on the top and on the side. Follow the line horizontally from the left until you reach the cells under time and go down four. That is four down and seven across. You have a time-per- diversity-hire combination to look at to see if there is a useful dependent measure there. Since your mind can quickly flip the equation back and forth between time-per-hire and hire-per-time, it is unnecessary to bother with duplicate cells. For that reason, the cells in the lower left half of the grid have been eliminated.

While focusing only on the top right side of the grid you still have every combination possible among the 10 variables. In a 7 X 7 grid, there are 49 cells. Through the procedure just described, we have eliminated cells without any loss of possibilities. What remain are possible combinations of variables that might be useful dependent measures. The next step is to match them.

Begin at the top left corner and proceed horizontally to the right, checking each cell for a useful combination. The first cell is the combination of cost (across) and recruiter (down). Is this a worthwhile measure? The answer is yes. Perhaps you could use the cost of maintaining a recruiter in some formula. Is it be useful to have the cost per hour of a recruiter to factor into a formula such as cost per hire? If you want to know the average cost of hiring new employees from diverse backgrounds, one of the cost components is labor cost. You need the fully burdened hourly rate of a recruiter multiplied by the average amount of time that you find your recruiters spend generating each diversity hire. Recruiter cost becomes useful as an independent measure in this example.

Diversity is a part of a system of organizational change. And as part of that system, it is made up of subsystems that feed other subsystems to create the whole. This is a minute example of that point. A variable or combination of variables may serve as either an independent variable or a dependent variable. The complexity of human resources in an organization becomes apparent when you look at it on the variable level. It is this complexity that has frightened off many who have tried to measure it. But, using the examples we will explore in this book, you will see that there is nothing to fear. If you reduce the diversity initiatives to their basic elements, namely the variables that make up the results or the processes that produce the outcomes, it becomes relatively easy to track the activity and discover the interactions.

Are either cost over time (C/T) or time over cost (T/C) worthwhile measures? Most would say yes. However, the answer is no because there is no context for what kind of cost or time we would measure. Cost per diversity hire or time to hire diverse candidates might make sense, but cost versus time alone is too amorphous. Hence, this cell is worthless. You have quickly learned that not all cells yield useful measures. If it helps you, it is useful; and if it doesn't, forget it and go on.

At this stage in the development of quantitative measurement for human resources, there are no generally accepted accounting principles. Choose whatever you want, and report whatever you like. The only rule that applies is to be consistent in your methodology and selection of independent variables.

Another cell in the matrix is diversity requisitions. The question is, what is the cost per diversity requisition? How much does your organization spend processing requisitions for diverse candidate hires? Do you care to know? Is it necessary to have this number as an independent variable in another formula? If the answer to all these questions is no, you can probably proceed to the next cell. How about calculating the cost per interview? This measure may have value as part of a cost per hire measure. For every diversity hire, there are often many interviews. If you want a very precise total cost of hiring, then you need to know the average cost per interview and the average number of interviews per hire.

You can also look at the total amount spent on ads, agencies, or other sources that target diverse candidate hires. You can run comparisons on a per-hire basis. You need them as components in a total cost-per-hire formula. They can also be used in combination with time. You can compare the average cost and the average time to fill a job using traditional ads versus agencies specializing in diverse candidate recruiting to make a business decision. You may trade off high cost for quick response if you have a critical job to fill. If there is no rush and you want to reduce expense, you can give up the better time source for the better cost source (assuming they are different).

You can run trials of cost against all other variables on the list. Some will be found to be necessary, others discretionary. The choices are yours and the people with whom you work. Simply start over on the next line. When you have finished this list of seven variables and potential measures, you will fully understand how to generate measures in any situation. The procedure is always the same: List the variables; matrix them on a grid; eliminate redundant and duplicate cells; match each variable against all other variables, one at a time; and then make decisions as to each combination's usefulness.

The matrix method produces more potential measurement variables than you need. The only question is, "Which one to use now?"

CREATING FORMULAS

YOU HAVE NOW CREATED A NUMBER OF DEPENDENT VARIABLES, but there are still some tasks to be done. This is not the end, but, rather, the beginning. These measures can only be realized if the independent variables that comprise them are identified and put into a formula. If we use a complex measure like cost per diversity hire (C/DH) as an example, the process is quite easy to understand.

There are two basic components to this measure: cost and diversity hires. First identify all the cost elements. There are advertising charges (AC), agency fees (AF), bonuses to employees for referrals (in some companies) (RB), recruiter and clerical time costs (ST), client time costs (the manager with the job opening) (MT), overhead (OH), possibly travel and relocation expenses (T&R), and miscellaneous costs (Misc).

These symbols are shown below in equation form.

$$AC+AF+RB+ST+MT+OH+T\&R+Misc$$

After you are satisfied that you have accounted for all cost items, draw a line under them, and go to the diversity hiring issue. This is simple. It is the number of diverse candidates hired during the time period that the expenses were incurred. It is expressed as DH.

$$\frac{AC+AF+RB+ST+MT+OH+T\&R+Misc}{DH}$$

This completes the ratio but not the equation. To do that, add the dependent measure C/DH in front.

$$C/DH = \frac{AC+AF+RB+ST+MT+OH+T\&R+Misc}{DH}$$

This gives you the total, or what is usually called the whole direct measure. It is whole because it includes all variables and accounts for all diversity hires. It is direct because it can be directly related to costs of operating the organization. Direct measures are always identifiable by the fact that they are measuring some kind of cost. Indirect measures do not cover cost, but do describe some measure of time (which can be converted to cost), quantity, or quality. Indirect measures, such as the number of mentoring sessions held, or the number of trainee hours of diversity instruction conducted, also have value in the attempt to understand and evaluate how effectively a diversity initiative is being implemented.

While whole measures are very beneficial for management and the diversity steering organization, they are often too simplistic for problem-identification or problem-solving purposes. To fully differentiate activity and results among groups, it is necessary to subdivide the data. For example, cost-per-diversity-hire numbers can be subdivided by:

- Source of hire

- Level of hire

- Occupational groups

- Departments or divisions

- Time periods

As we discuss specific measures throughout the remainder of the book, you will see examples of how this adds meaning to the numbers.

ADVANCED METHODS: THE FAMILY OF MEASURES

THERE IS A TENDENCY TO SEARCH FOR SINGLE-ANSWER MODELS for measuring the success of diversity or other types of human resources processes or programs. In fact, an excellent organization needs to monitor a range of variables. This range or family of variables can include quality, productivity and financial return.

The creation of a measurement system cannot be a mechanical modeling exercise. It must be preceded by an inspection of basic principles and of organizational and departmental strategic thinking, as well as by an assessment of desired quality of work-life. Developing the actual measures is easily compared to the amount of time that should be spent thinking about what is important to the organization's diversity initiatives and the expectations of the measurement activity.

WHY A "FAMILY" OF MEASURES?

THERE ARE THREE BASIC USES OF ANY KIND OF PERFORMANCE measurement: control, screening, and planning. Control measures (*i.e.*, number of diverse hires per month), for example, tend to be simple, physical (as opposed to financial), and frequent. Planning measures (*i.e.*, cost of diverse hires by agency source) tend to be complex, financial, and infrequent. Screening (or diagnosis) measures (*i.e.*, cost of diverse hire voluntary terminations) fall between the two. An excellent control measure is usually a poor planning measure and vice versa. A successful diversity measurement effort will have plenty of each kind of performance measurement, not just one.

The Family of Measures method allows you to predetermine goals for each of the family members and give points along a 0-10 scale as improvement is made. Each member of the family is weighted according to priority. Then the weighted performance scores of the members are aggregated to a single performance score for the diversity initiative, the department, the unit, and the organization. The overall results can be used for general motivational purposes, whereas the individual measures are used more diagnostically.

Here are a few of the types of measures frequently included in such a family:

Measure Type	Description
Productivity	• Productivity is the relationship between the amount of one or more inputs and the amount of output from a clearly identified process. The most common measure is labor productivity, which is the amount of labor input (such as labor hours or employees) per physical unit of measured output. This type of measure is helpful when examining the productivity of diverse work teams compared to homogeneous work teams. • Cost of service usually measures productivity. It might include the sum of several variable costs associated with the delivery of service. For example, comparative variable cost of service delivery using diverse employee resources matching customer groups and markets versus cost of service delivery using traditional employee resources in diverse customer markets.
Quality	• Quality pertains to both the adequacy of processing within an organization and the characteristics of what is delivered outside the organization. One aspect of quality (customer satisfaction) deals with whether the service rendered is what the outside customer expected,

Measure Type	Description
	wanted, or specified. Some of the measures of customer satisfaction, especially regarding services, are quite subjective. They appear as post-audit reviews, complaints, or satisfaction surveys. This type of measure is useful when assessing diverse work group and customer satisfaction with the organization.
Utilization	• Utilization of the measure of resources used versus resources available for use. Although utilization is usually regarded as equipment, it is also important in human resources. How well and how often diverse human resources are used to address organizational issues or their lack of use can make a difference in the organization's ability to be effective (*i.e.*, in diverse consumer markets, where the organization has virtually no presence but could if diverse talents were used to bring their experience and background to bear on the problem).
Creativity or Innovation	• Some staffs (particularly advertising agencies and research labs) are required to be creative and innovative, but usually within structured objectives. In other instances, work teams are often asked to come up with creative and innovative solutions to organizational problems and issues. The work of Dr. Taylor Cox, University of Michigan, *et.al.*, has presented definitive evidence that diverse work teams are often more innovative, creative, and productive than homogeneous work teams. Thus, measures of this type can be helpful. Overall, it is difficult to measure creativity and innovation directly, though people seem to "know it when they see it." Therefore, sensitive interviewing of experts as to the tangible manifestations of creativity

Measure Type	Description
	can often lead to some fairly direct measures. There are also indirect measures, such as awards received, publications, or other externally driven recognition achieved.
Outcome	• Sometimes the direct output of a process may be fairly trivial or difficult to measure, but downstream and later in time there is an ultimate outcome that can be measured. For example, installing a day-care facility on-site for employees and its impact on absenteeism, productivity, and diverse employee retention.

HOW TO CONSTRUCT A FAMILY OF MEASURES
OBJECTIVES MATRIX

The procedure that follows outlines the process for constructing a Family of Measures Objectives Matrix. The example illustrates a family of measures with four interrelated, yet separate, aspects of performance within the hiring and staffing department covering diverse employee hiring and retention. The measures were created after group reflection on the organization's mission, products, services, customers, and objectives.

Dimension	Description
Function	➤ Hiring and staffing
Mission	➤ To acquire, retain, and promote the best and brightest workforce talent available.
Objectives	➤ Increase by 25% the percentage of African American and Filipino workforce members in engineering and technical computer trades

Dimension	Description
	➤ Retain female candidates beyond the 3-year mark ➤ Increase by 25% the diverse applicant flow for Hispanics and African Americans ➤ Reduce by 20% the turnover of females ➤ Increase by 15% the pool of promotion-eligible minorities for all managerial levels
Candidates for Family of Measures	➤ Number of females and minorities hired versus previous year's actual ➤ Number of females and minorities hired versus percentage in the applicant flow ➤ Number of females and minorities hired versus percentages of area availability as determined by EEOC data ➤ Turnover of females and minorities versus percentage for white males ➤ Turnover of females and minorities versus previous year's trend line ➤ Turnover of females and minorities versus external benchmark ➤ Percentage of promotion-ready minority employees by level (age, race, sex, education, salary grade, performance level, job classification) ➤ Survival/loss rate of new hires ➤ Termination rate by reason for leaving
Final (weighted) family of Measures	➤ Percentage of promotion-ready minority employees by level (age, race, sex, education, salary grade, performance level, job classification) (40%) ➤ Survival/loss rate of new diverse hires (30%) ➤ Termination rate by reason for leaving: lack of career opportunities (15%) ➤ Number of females and minorities hired versus percentage in the applicant flow (15%)

Once the basic family of measures have been identified, the following steps should be completed to create the Family of Measures Index.

Step 1: Develop an appropriate family of measures for the diversity initiative, department, or process to be measured. Four to six distinct measures is normal. Some of them may be interrelated, but perceived differently by different people, which means they can be measured differently.

Step 2: Insert those measures as column heads on the Objectives Matrix grid. Develop a weighting of the relative importance of those measures that adds to 100 percent and insert those values in the row identified as weight. Though all of the measures are important, the example will emphasize the number of promotion-ready minority employees by level and the survival/loss rate.

FAMILY OF MEASURES METHOD					
Productivity Criteria	Promotion-Ready Minority Employees by Level	Survival/ Loss Rate of New Hires	Termination Rate/Lack of Career Opportunity	Females and Minorities Hired vs. Applicant Flow	Etc
Performance	33	71	20	30	
Target Value	10	49	94	5	55
	9	45	89	8	49
	8	41	83	11	45
	7	37	77	14	41
	6	33	71	17	37
Values	5	29	66	19	33
	4	25	61	21	29
Base Value	3	21	56	23	25
	2	17	51	25	21
	1	13	46	27	17
	0	10	41	29	13
Score		6.0	6.0	4.8	4.2
Weight		40	30	15	15
Value		240	180	72	63
INDEX:		555 *			

* This index score is 555 points out of a possible perfect score of 1,000.

Step 3: Calculate or assume a base value for each measure. The base may be the value of the most recent quarter or year, a current standard, or a long-term average. It might even be an intelligent guess, if the measurement effort is just starting. The base value should be inserted in row 3.

Step 4: Develop as collaboratively as possible a target or goal for a future time period (three years from now, for example) for each measure. Insert those values in row 10. The amount of effort required to go from the base number in row 3 to the goal in row 10 should be comparable for each column—not in absolute numbers or percent, but rather in overall difficulty of each challenge.

Step 5: Fill in the values in each column for rows 4 through 9. If the difficulty of going from one level of performance to another is linear, then the progression of the values could be geometric. If the compounded growth rate required to go from row 3's value to row 10's value is 8 percent, then each value in the column would increase about 8 percent. A simple way to work these numbers is to use a straight line on semi-log graph paper. If, however, the "going gets tougher" as you approach row 10's target, a curvelinear pattern is appropriate. For example, the increment between rows 3 and 4 might be a 12 percent increase, followed by 10 percent, 8 percent, and so on, to where the increment between rows 9 and 10 is only 3 percent. This is found in measures that approach 100 percent, such as a customer satisfaction score or a diverse employee survival rate score.

Step 6: Fill in the values from rows 2 to 0 using the same logic as in step 5. Recognize that going substantially below the 0 value may force starting over, so think of the 0 value as intolerable or outrageously bad.

Step 7: Eventually the first new measuring occurs in a month, a quarter, or even a year (quarterly is usually recommended.) Insert the actual values in the Performance row. Locate those values in their respective columns and read the corresponding value or score from the row numbers. In general, it will be necessary to interpolate between whole row numbers. Thus, if row 5's total value is 157 and row 4's total value is 149, an actual value of 152 would earn an approximate score of 4.4 (4.0 + 3/8 of 1.0). Insert the interpolated score in the row called Value.

Step 8: Multiply the score by the weight in each column and place those results in the Value row. Add across the values numbers and put the total in the index box. That is the final score for the family of measures for the current time period. Assuming reasonable consistency in the amount of "stretch" from 3 to 10 in each department and/or process being measured, the absolute scores can be roughly compared across the organization as indicators of progress even though the specific measures will normally be quite different.

Though it may take a bit more time, the Family of Measures is an excellent method for providing an aggregate and motivational evaluation of your organization's diversity initiatives.

FOCUS ON RESULTS

TODAY'S WATCHWORDS ARE MANAGEMENT BY FACT, and it is up to the diversity professional to answer the challenge by providing appropriate facts through the use of a variety of measurement methods (such as those discussed in this chapter). It is important to remember that measures and measurement are primarily a means to an end, which is achieving results!

Results are the variable that will make or break a diversity effort. If the initiative is focused on diversity hires, management will want to know: What did it cost? How much time did it take? How many diversity hires did the effort generate during the measurement period? What was the quality of the hires? How did this effort impact organizational profitability? These things are critical.

When you can prove that the diversity effort has achieved positive results in key areas, you help establish diversity as an important factor in the organization's success.

5 Organizing Your Measures: The Diversity 9-S Framework

APPLYING A STRATEGIC LINK TO THE ORGANIZATION

DIVERSITY IMPACTS VIRTUALLY EVERY ASPECT of the organization. Diversity-related activities in many organizations run on parallel tracks, often encompassing different departments, individuals, processes, and strategic objectives. It is important to recognize these links because changing to a more inclusive, diverse workforce is not a fad-of-the-day program. It is a complete culture change process! Therefore, it not only impacts organizational training programs but the organization's vision, values, policies, procedures, management practices, systems, standards of operation, reward methods, recruitment strategies, and organizational structure.

Diversity initiatives proceed along the same lines as other key business strategies and objectives (such as changes in marketing approach, operational strategies, financial tactics, and culture.) and reflect vital similarities:

✔ They are grounded in business rationale.

  ➤ Motivated by competitive realities

  ➤ Often start with CEO or top management vision

☑ They stress empowerment management.

☑ They represent "way of life" changes in the corporate culture if the culture is to sustain itself.

> ➤ Comprehensive in scope, dozens of changes

> ➤ Need to be sustained over a number of years to complete an organizational transition and change

☑ They require long-term pioneering efforts involving:

> ➤ False starts, ups and downs

> ➤ Ambiguities that go with pioneering

> ➤ Discomfort in "lead steer" role

☑ They share similarity of implementation strategies.

> ➤ Visible, strong leadership

> ➤ Focus on customer results
>   · Internal first, then external
>   · Measure customer opinion

> ➤ Training of all employees
>   · Start with awareness, follow with skills
>   · Subjects in common: empowerment, communications, team/group dynamics

> ➤ Recognition of participation and contribution

> ➤ Communication of the effort

> ➤ Development of process, tools, and vocabulary to implement change

> ➤ Valuing and utilizing diverse input to develop more new ideas for improvement

Coordinating these activities and their measurement permits the greatest influence and impact on the organization's strategic direction, especially when budgets and other organizational resources are slim. For example, some potential areas of overlap in measuring diversity initiatives include the following:

- Measuring the presence of a shared diversity mission within the organization

- Determining whether there is organizational support for diversity values

- Examining whether policies, procedures, systems, regulations, structure, and rules are supportive of or in conflict with diversity initiatives.

- Analyzing whether diversity training programs are making a difference in the participants and the performance of the organization

- Measuring the impact of diverse work employees on increasing representation in workforce planning and succession planning efforts

The scope of potential diversity measurement activities and the similarity of effort underscore the point that diversity initiatives and measurement should be a normal and natural part of the way an organization does business.

The Diversity 9-S Framework helps organizations examine holistically their diversity change efforts to ensure alignment with key organizational variables. The measurements serve as lenses for viewing and measuring an organization's diversity implementation effectiveness. When combined, they offer a powerful, integrated, strategic approach for managing a diversity culture change process.

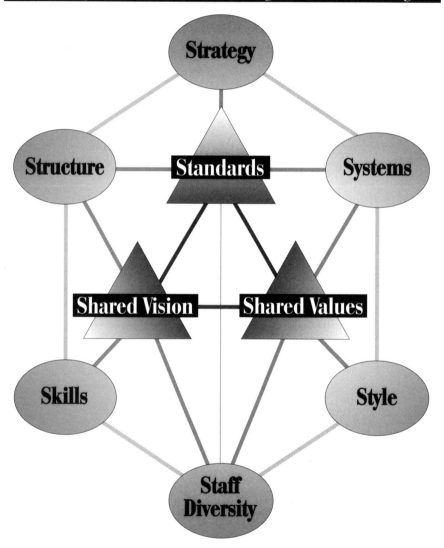

Diversity 9-S Framework for Organizational Change

Strategy

Structure

Standards

Systems

Shared Vision

Shared Values

Skills

Style

Staff Diversity

The Diversity 9-S Framework consist of the following elements:

SHARED VISION

THIS ELEMENT IS A MUTUALLY DERIVED STRATEGIC direction among employees, management, and the organization's customers. It reflects the organization's aspirations, purpose, goals, and objectives. It is represented by a visual image of a desired future for the organization to meet the strategic needs of its stakeholders.

When measuring this dimension of the Diversity 9-S Framework, it is important to examine:

- The clarity of the diversity vision for the organization and its key stakeholders

- The presence of an organizational visual image illustrating the desired future state in pictures, images, sounds, and feelings that will be in place once this future state is achieved

- How thoroughly diversity initiatives are being supported, and what can be done to further achievement of the diversity vision

SHARED VALUES

THIS ELEMENT REQUIRES RE-EXAMINATION OF ORGANIZATIONAL values and culture or the "guiding and daily beliefs." It offers an opportunity to interpret values and identity and bridge any gaps between espoused values and individual behavior. This requires an investment of time and resources.

Top management must make a commitment to ensure that values related to diversity are clearly understood and practiced by all. If the principle values of leveraging diversity are in place and operating, they will be seen in what people do, not what's written in a brochure about your culture.

When measuring this element of the Diversity 9-S Framework, it is important to examine:

- The decisions and policies that illustrate these values

- The rewards and how they relate to stated diversity initiatives

- The values and organizational actions that illustrate their use day-to-day

STANDARDS

THIS ELEMENT INCLUDES CONCISE, MEASURABLE success factors that apply to all aspects of the organizational framework. It provides consistent feedback on how well the organization is meeting its diversity commitments to all stakeholders during and after the transition and change process. The diversity standards dimension is the benchmark of the effort.

Organization systems that are highly accountable require that each system be supported by critical success factors that reflect changes to the organization and its customers.

When measuring this dimension of the Diversity 9-S Framework, it is important to examine:

- The need for tracking systems to be in place and agreed to

- Hard and soft diversity measures of performance in place and valued as evidenced by a visible reward system

- Best practices identified and benchmarked

- "Report card" and/or "mental model" diversity measures in place and utilized to measure effectiveness at the activity, process, outcome, impact and value-added levels.

STRATEGY

THIS ELEMENT INCLUDES TACTICS, PLANS AND integrating mechanisms for business objectives, as well as plans and programs that relate to valuing and leveraging diversity. An organization's marketing, financial, and operations strategies have direct linkages to the full utilization of its human resources.

Effectively utilizing this element in a diversity change effort requires that each organization have a "human capital plan" that is every bit as strategic as the allocation of its business capital. Opportunities abound for organizations that make explicit, concrete connections between the goals of the organization and the effective management and leveraging of diverse workforce resources.

When measuring this dimension of the Diversity 9-S Framework, it is important to identify and examine:

- Diversity work practices that leverage the talents and skills of diverse work teams

- The groups that influence strategy formulation and monitoring the requirements for diverse workforce representation and input

- Formal business strategies to determine if they are built to capitalize on diverse workforce resources to meet competitive and other organizational needs

STRUCTURE

THIS ELEMENT MAKES CERTAIN THAT THE PROPER ORGANIZATION structural framework is in place to support an inclusive work environment. Are new reporting relationship structures needed within the organization to convey the sense of urgency, accountability, and importance for utilizing the talents of the diverse workforce?

Are new task forces, advisory committees, or self-directed teams needed to address and direct attention to diversity issues and the way diverse workforce needs are addressed?

Changes in the organization chart and its structure send a loud message about who and what are important.

When measuring this dimension of the Diversity 9-S Framework, it is important to examine:

· Whether operational and team structures are designed to support diversity

· Whether integrating mechanisms exist for problem solving and information sharing using workforce diversity.

SYSTEMS

THIS ELEMENT INCLUDES SUCH ORGANIZATIONAL COMPONENTS as recruitment and hiring practices, training and development policies, promotion and succession rules, performance appraisal regulations, and compensation practices. Each must be examined to determine congruency with the organization's diversity imperatives.

In essence, all policies, practices, rules, regulations, and procedures that employees follow to perform job-related duties must be examined for possible change.

When measuring this dimension of the Diversity 9-S Framework, it is important to examine:

• How policies, procedures, rules, and regulations are designed to support the diversity change effort

• Whether different modes of decision making, problem-solving, and communication are used to manage and leverage diversity.

SKILLS

THIS ELEMENT REPRESENTS THE TALENTS AND ABILITIES of the workforce that can give an organization its competitive advantage. The relationship between the skills an organization possesses in managing and leveraging diversity and the bottom-line gains achieved go hand-in-hand.

Leveraging the rich talents of a diverse work group can add exponentially to an organization's quality of output and productivity. Employee and management skills for working in a diverse work environment must be valued as a competitive organizational asset.

When measuring this dimension of the Diversity 9-S Framework, it is important to examine:

• Whether core diversity competencies are in place and evaluated for all levels of employees

- Whether Level 3 evaluation (skill transfer) methods are in place and fully utilized to gauge whether participants are applying the diversity awareness and skills while carrying out their job

STYLE

THIS ELEMENT INCLUDES THE DAY-TO-DAY MANAGEMENT and leadership behavior that ultimately creates the climate of the organization (in other words, "what it's like to work here"). Style represents a major force that models the priorities of the organization in everyday behavior. It can be seen in how management and leaders of the organization facilitate the process of organizational performance. It is reflected in how people are treated and the level of acceptance of differences that prevails.

The organization's style must reflect a strong sensitivity and practice for effectively utilizing a diverse workforce in pursuit of organizational objectives.

When measuring this dimension of the Diversity 9-S Framework, it is important to examine:

- The degree to which prevailing managerial practices and styles are supportive of workforce diversity

- How current cultural practices support diversity (rites, mentoring, rituals, ceremony)

STAFF

THIS ELEMENT INCLUDES A PROFILE OF THE EMPLOYEE BODY or the types of people residing (and where) in the organization. Information about the organization's primary and secondary dimensions of diversity must be known and leveraged.

A typical misconception is that many more women and minorities reside in the organization across functions and at higher levels. Staying informed of the organization's workforce statistics, as well as current and future labor needs, will assist everyone in responding to the challenges of a diverse organizational and customer marketplace.

When measuring this dimension of the Diversity 9-S Framework, it is important to examine:

- Whether the employee base reflects the target diversity mix at all levels

- What groups are under-represented

- What staffing requirements are needed to meet national or global competitive needs

CREATING AN INTEGRATED PICTURE OF THE DIVERSITY EFFORT

ALL OF THESE ELEMENTS MUST OPERATE INTERDEPENDENTLY to develop high levels of synergy and to provide an integrated view of the organization's performance. The graphic that follows highlights the Diversity 9-S measures which will be discussed throughout the book:

Category	Measurement
Core Elements	
Shared Vision	• Diversity Vision/Mission Written • # of times Diversity mentioned as strategy in executive presentations

Category	Measurement
	• % change in local and global customer diversity demographic versus prior five years • % change in local and global employee diversity demographics versus prior five years as compared to benchmarked leaders in industry • Gross productivity % versus prior five year period
Shared Values	• Diversity Values written with behaviorally specific descriptions • % Diversity Values training conducted • # of times Diversity Values mentioned in executive presentations • Survey rating of values installation
Standards	• Family of Diversity measures method • Diversity Best Practices compiled, taught, and measured
Basic Elements	
Strategy	• Diversity Business Rationale Strategy Written • # of times Diversity Business Rationale mentioned as a strategy to accomplish the organization's business objectives • % of Diversity Goals Attained • # of Diversity specific goals completed by department • # of Diversity specific goals assigned by department
Structure	• Degree of Variation by Diversity Dimension • # of Diverse Work Teams by Strategic Result Area • # of Departmental or Divisional Differences Represented on a Team • # of Levels of Management Represented on a Team • # of Geographical Differences Represented on a Team

Category	Measurement
Systems	· Diversity tied to management compensation
	· # and Type of Policies and Procedures Assessed for Diverse Workforce Impact
	· # and Type of Policies and Procedures Changed for Diversity Impact
	· Absence Rate
	· Absenteeism Cost
	· Average Hourly Rate
	· % Gender Based Pay Differential
	· Effect of Absenteeism on Labor Utilization
	· Diversity Performance Appraisal Metrics
Skills	· Reaction Level
	· Reaction Evaluation Tool
	· Learning Level
	· Pre/Post Self-assessment Tool
	· Short-answer Evaluation Tool
	· Knowledge Change Score
	· Skill (Behavior) Change Score
	· Attitude Change Score
	· Behavior Level
	· Post Training Survey for Participants
	· Post Training Survey for Managers
	· Diversity Behavior Checklist Tool
	· Results Level
	· Results-focused Questionnaire Tool
	· Return-on-Investment Level (ROI)
	· ROI Calculation
	· ROE Calculation
	· Cost-Benefit Calculation

Category	Measurement
Staff	• Time-to-Fill
	• Cost per Diversity Hire.
	• Source Cost per Diversity Hire
	• Diversity Hit Rate
	• Diversity Hire Referral Rate
	• Diversity Hire Performance Impact
	• Average Tenure by Diversity Grouping versus Former Employees
	• Diversity Stability Factor, Diversity Instability Factor
	• Diversity Survivor Rate, Diversity Loss Rate
Style	• Employee Opinion Survey—Diversity elements
	• Stratified Focus Group Feedback
	• % favorable responses on Organizational Culture Audit as compared to previous years, other parts of the organization and industry
	• # of Minorities and Women in Management and Leadership Positions
	• 5x5 Study—5 years at level 5 performance
	• $ and % of Budget Allocated to Diversity Initiatives
	• Organizational Mentoring Analysis

To be effective, the diversity **shared vision** must be embraced by everyone, the **shared values** must be demonstrated in what people do, the **standards** must benchmark performance, the **structure** must be well-defined to foster inclusion, the **strategy** must utilize diverse workforce assets, all **systems** must reinforce organizational behavior that supports diversity initiatives, the level of diversity **skill** must be outstanding, the management and leadership **style** must facilitate collaboration and respect, and the staff should reflect diverse individuals well-suited for their job responsibilities. In order for an effective diversity initiative to make a measurable difference, the organization's "9-S" framework for diversity measurement must be created, implemented, and communicated.

In the chapters that follow, I will provide specific diversity measurements and step-by-step, how-to methods for organizing and measuring your diversity results using the Diversity 9-S Framework. Each chapter will focus on a specific aspect of the Diversity 9-S Framework and highlight appropriate measures supporting that dimension.

6 Diversity Shared Vision, Shared Values, and Standards: Establishing Core System Measures

INTRODUCTION

IF THE DIVERSITY CHANGE PROCESS DEMANDS A SYSTEMATIC approach to measurement, then your first order of business is to establish a core set of diversity metrics. At bare minimum, the system should gauge how well the diversity vision is shared, the diversity values are understood and practiced, and monitor essential diversity performance standards to sustain the effort.

MEASURES TO SUPPORT THESE DIMENSIONS: DIVERSITY VISION, VALUES, AND STANDARDS

THE FOLLOWING DIVERSITY MEASURES WILL BE DISCUSSED in this chapter (they are not intended to be exhaustive, but instead reflect some possible measures to use in each area):

Shared Vision Measures

1. Diversity vision/mission written

2. Number of times diversity mentioned as strategy in executive presentations

3. Percent change in local and global customer diversity demographics versus trends of past three or five years

4. Percent change in local and global employee diversity demographics versus prior three or five years as compared to benchmark leaders in industry (Note: this may be purely a function of recruitment approaches, e.g., only hire and recruit from similar sources, therefore no diverse workforce hires in the workplace)

5. Gross productivity percent versus prior three or five year period (gross revenue / average number of employees *versus prior three years)*

Shared Values Measures

1. Diversity values written with behaviorally specific descriptions

2. Number of times diversity values mentioned in executive presentations

3. Percent diversity values training completed

4. Survey rating of values installation

Standards Measures

1. Family of diversity measures method

2. Diversity best practices compiled, taught, and measured

APPLYING MEASURES TO YOUR SITUATION

THE TRUE VALUE OF A MEASUREMENT SYSTEM BECOMES APPARENT only when you understand each component of the formula and apply the measure(s) to your specific situation. In this chapter and the chapters that follow, diversity measures for each of the Diversity 9-S Framework segments will be presented using the following general analysis format as appropriate:

· Diversity measure

· Measure description

· Suggested use/purpose

· Additional analyses

· Formula elements

· Formula example

· Key analysis or processing questions to examine for this measure

The following analysis for the diversity measure Source Cost per Diversity Hire illustrates how this format will be applied to the diversity measures explored throughout the book:

ELEMENT	APPLICATION
Diversity Measure	Source Cost per Diversity Hire (SCDH)
Measure Description	This measure highlights the cost of diversity hires based upon the sources used to find those hires (*e.g.*, agencies, churches, ethnic/professional associations).
Suggested Use /Purpose	To measure the staffing element of the Diversity 9-S Framework, examine the performance level of the recruiting organization.
Additional Analyses	By level (exempt vs. non-exempt or management level), average, mode, median, diversity groupings (such race and gender).
Formula Elements	SC/DH = AC + AF + RB + NC DH *Where*: • AC = advertising costs, total monthly expenditure (*e.g.*, $28,000) • AF = agency fee, total month (*e.g.*, $19,000) • RB = referral bonuses, total paid (*e.g.*, $2,300) • NC = no-cost hires, walk-ins, non-profit agencies, etc. (*e.g.*, $0) • DH = Total Diversity hires (119)
Example	$$SC/DH = \frac{\$28,000 + \$19,000+\$2300+\$0}{119}$$ $$= \frac{\$49,300}{119}$$ $$= \$415$$

ELEMENT	APPLICATION
Key Analysis or Processing Questions to Examine for this Measure	1. What is the cost?
	2. How does it compare with this same period last year, last month, Over the last three years? Why?
	3. Is the trend going down, up, staying the same? Why?
	4. How does this trend or figure compare with others in our industry? Our competition?
	5. What are the business implications and consequences of this number based upon the organization's strategic objectives?
	6. How does this number compare with best practices standards for this type of data?
	7. What should our next steps be in light of this information? Why? When? Who? How? What barriers exist?

Now, let's explore the measures that support the diversity vision, values, and standards dimension of the Diversity 9-S Framework.

ANALYZING THE DIVERSITY SHARED VISION DIMENSION

THE FOLLOWING INFORMATION PROVIDES AN OVERVIEW of the diversity measures and associated formulas that can be used to monitor the Diversity Shared Vision dimension of the organization.

Shared Vision Measure-1

ELEMENT	APPLICATION
Diversity Measure	Diversity Vision/Mission Written

ELEMENT	APPLICATION
Measure Description	This is simply a measure that benchmarks whether the organization has invested the time and effort to thoughtfully craft a vision or mission statement for the organization.
Suggested Use/Purpose	To unite the organization's employees in valuing and managing diversity to support its strategic business objectives. The completion of this task should be listed as a milestone item within the strategic business plan.
Formula	There is no formula *per se* for this measure other than the presence or absence of the shared diversity vision. However, this task should be listed as a milestone item in the strategic plan with input and participation from the full organization. A representative body such as a diversity steering committee or diversity advisory board with a cross-section of the employee base can serve as a resource to help formulate a draft and the final vision document.

Shared Vision Measure-2

ELEMENT	APPLICATION
Diversity Measure	**Number of Times Diversity Mentioned as a Strategy to Accomplish the Organization's Business Objectives**
Measure Description	This is a "soft" measure to gauge whether the diversity vision is being supported in executive presentations.
Suggested Use/Purpose	To unite the organization's employees in valuing and managing diversity to support its strategic business objectives.

ELEMENT	APPLICATION
Formula	There is no formula. The entity responsible for monitoring the organization's commitment to diversity can periodically scan executive and other communications to employees and other audiences regarding diversity's role in the organization's business strategy.

Shared Vision Measure-3

ELEMENT	APPLICATION
Diversity Measure	**Percent Change in Local or Global Customer Diversity Demographics vs Past 3-5 Years**
Measure Description	This measure highlights changes in customer diversity demographics over a specified period of time. If the organization's shared diversity vision is to be effective, it must contain an accurate assessment of its changing diversity marketplace.
Suggested Use/Purpose	To measure the shared vision element of the Diversity 9-S Framework, examine the organization's changing diversity marketplace and track emerging market trends.
Formula Elements	$$\% \, \mathbf{ChgDCM} = \frac{\text{CDCM1} + \text{CDCM2} + \text{CDCM3} + \text{etc.}}{N}$$ Where: • CDCM1 = change in diversity customer market #1 (*e.g.*, 32%) • Note: This calculation requires that you track the number of customers in a particular market segment by diversity dimension (*e.g.*, age, race, or gender) for the time specified. For example, if you were interested in tracking the change in

ELEMENT	APPLICATION
	gender statistics in one segment of your customer market you would need to calculate: (# key customer contacts by gender added in that segment during the period / average # key customer contacts by gender in that customer market segment during the period)*100. The average # key customer contacts is used since 2-3 new customer contacts may have changed at one location during the period (*i.e.*, over a month's time). This could have happened at several customer offices that are a part of the total customer market segment. **Example:** If you had 27 new female key customer contacts added during the period and the average number of female key contacts was 84 for the month of March, then the percent change for that diversity customer market segment for the month of March was: $(27/84)*100 = 32\%$ • CDCM2 = change in diversity customer market #2 (*e.g.*, 25%) • CDCM3 = change in diversity customer market #3 (*e.g.*, 10%) • N = number of indicators used (*e.g.*, 3)
Example (assumes 3 customer markets total)	$$\%ChgDCM = \frac{32 + 25 + 10}{3}$$ $$= \frac{67}{3}$$ $$= 22.3\%$$
Key Analysis or Processing Questions to Examine for this Measure	1. How does it compare with this same period last year, last month, over the last three years? Why? 2. Is the trend going down, up, staying the same? Why? 3. How does this trend or figure compare with others in our industry? Our competition?

ELEMENT	APPLICATION
	4. What are the business implications and consequences of this number based upon the organization's strategic objectives? 5. What should our next steps be in light of this information? Why? When? Who? How? What barriers exist?
Possible Graphic	

Shared Vision Measure-4

ELEMENT	APPLICATION
Diversity Measure	**Percent Change in Local or Global Employee Diversity Demographics vs. Past 3-5 Years**
Measure	This measure highlights changes in employee diversity demographics over a specified period of time. If the organization's shared diversity vision is to be effective, it must contain an accurate assessment of its changing diversity workplace.
Suggested Use/Purpose	To measure the shared vision element of the Diversity 9-S Framework, examine the organization's changing diversity workplace and track emerging competitive market trends.
Formula Elements	$$\% \text{ ChgEDWP} = \frac{\text{CEDWP1} + \text{CEDWP2} + \text{CEDWP3} + \text{etc.}}{N}$$ Where: • CEDWP1 = change in employee diversity, workplace #1 (*e.g.*, 32%)

ELEMENT	APPLICATION
	· **Note**: This calculation requires that you track the number of diverse employees in a particular workplace by diversity dimension (*e.g.*, age, race, and gender) for the time specified. For example, to track the change in gender statistics in a particular workplace, you need to calculate: (# employees by gender added during the period / average # employees by gender in that workplace during the period)*100. The average # employees is used since 2-3 new employees may have been hired and left a location during the period (*i.e.*, more than a month). This could have happened at several office locations that are a part of your total organization's population. **Example**: If you had 27 new female employees added during the period and the average number of female employees was 84 for the month of March, then the percent change for that workforce location in March was: (27/84)*100 = 32% · CEDWP2 = change in employee diversity, workplace #2 (*e.g.*, 25%) · CEDWP3 = change in employee diversity, workplace #3 (*e.g.*, 10%) N = number of indicators used (*e.g.*, 3)
Example (Assumes 3 Employee Workplace Locations)	$$\%ChgEDWP = \frac{32 + 25 + 10}{3}$$ $$= \frac{67}{3}$$ $$= 22.3\%$$

ELEMENT	APPLICATION
Key Analysis or Processing Questions to Examine for this Measure	1. How does it compare with this same period last year, last month, Over the last three years? Why? 2. Is the trend going down, up, staying the same? Why? 3. How does this trend or figure compare with others in our industry? Our competition? 4. What are the business implications and consequences of this number based upon the organization's strategic objectives? 5. What should our next steps be in light of this information? Why? When? Who? How? What barriers exist?
Possible Graphic	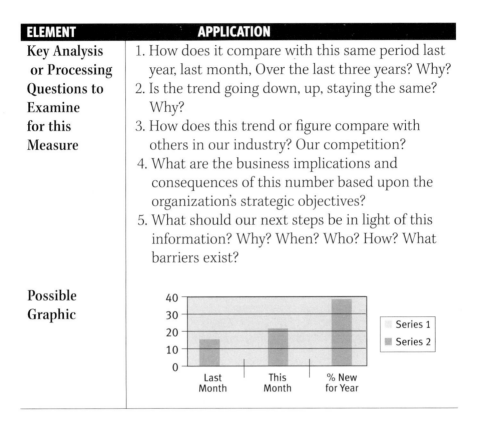

Shared Vision Measure-5

ELEMENT	APPLICATION
Measure	**Gross Productivity Dollars Per Employee vs. Prior Three Years**
Measure Description	This measure reflects the gross human asset productivity (measured in dollars) generated by the organization's workforce. Typically, this is represented as a comparative statistic over a three- to five-year period.
Suggested Use/Purpose	To gain an overall picture of the amount of revenue generated per employee. Caution: This measure is a broad picture measure. It takes into account all organizational events and consequences in which

ELEMENT	APPLICATION
	organizational revenues were produced (both controllable and non-controllable). Its true value is in examining trends over time and assessing its direction for further study
Additional Analyses	By level (exempt vs. non-exempt or management level). Note: It is often helpful to estimate what percentage of the gross revenue was affected by uncontrollable factors and create a weighted revenue number that more accurately reflects personnel generated revenues.
Formula Elements	**(Gross Revenue/Average Number Employees vs. Prior Five Years)** $$\$GR/E = \frac{YR1 + YR2 + YR3}{E}$$ Where: • $\$GR/E$ = dollar gross revenue per employee • YR1 = year one revenues (*e.g.*, \$10,658,000). Also true for YR2 (*e.g.*, \$17,120,000), YR3 (*e.g.*, \$25, 896,000). • E = average number of employees (*e.g.*, 3,097)
Example	$$\$GR/E = \frac{\$10,658,000}{2840} + \frac{\$17,120,000}{2976} + \frac{\$25,896,000}{3097}$$ $$= \quad \$3752.82 \qquad \$5752.69 \qquad \$8361.64$$ **Year 1** **Year 2** **Year 3** These numbers are read as ratios such as \$3,753:1 (employee). If this number improves significantly from year to year, it might be a sign that gross productivity is increasing. The improvement is not necessarily all in factory or operational productivity. It might be that salespeople are becoming more efficient or that a diverse engineering team has simplified a design or that manufacturing has an automated procedure. The reason is not

ELEMENT	APPLICATION
	necessarily obvious, but the result is clearly positive. Of course, a decrease in the number indicates a deterioration in performance somewhere. In a service business, higher productivity usually means that the organization is able to serve an increasing number of customers without adding staff. Overall, this figure is helpful in monitoring trends.
Key Analysis or Processing Questions to Examine for this Measure	1. What is the cost per year per employee? 2. How does it compare with this same period last year, last month, Over the last three years? Why? 3. Is the trend going down, up, staying the same? Why? 4. How does this trend or figure compare with others in our industry? Our competition? 5. What are the business implications and consequences of this number based upon the organization's strategic objectives? 6. How does this number compare with best practices standards for this type of data? 7. What should our next steps be in light of this information? Why? When? Who? How? What barriers exist?
Possible Graphic	**Sample Measure Chart** Dollars per Employee (10000, 8000, 6000, 4000, 2000, 0) — Years (1, 2, 3) — Series 1

ANALYZING THE DIVERSITY SHARED VALUES DIMENSION

THE FOLLOWING INFORMATION PROVIDES AN OVERVIEW of the diversity measures and associated formulas that can be used to monitor the diversity shared values dimension of the organization.

Shared Values Measure-1

ELEMENT	APPLICATION
Diversity Measure	Diversity Values Written
Measure Description	This is simply a measure that benchmarks whether the organization has invested the time and effort to thoughtfully craft a values statement for the organization.
Suggested Use/Purpose	To state key organizational values in behaviorally specific terms that describe behavioral expectations the organization has regarding workforce diversity. Implementation and completion of this task should be listed as a milestone item within the strategic business plan.
Formula	There is no formula *per se* for this measure other than the presence or absence of the set of diversity values. However, as stated above, this task should be listed as a milestone in the strategic plan with input and participation from the full organization. A representative body, such as a diversity steering committee or diversity advisory board with a cross-section of the employee base, can serve as a resource to help formulate a draft and the final values document.

ELEMENT	APPLICATION	
Sample Format	*Diversity Value*	*Actions Necessary to Support Value*
	1. Teamwork Across Diverse Work Groups	**1.1** Utilize self-directed diverse work teams extensively
		1.2 Reward team and team member behavior via the appraisal system and special recognition
		1.3 Set benchmark score for teamwork across diverse work groups on employee survey. Compare with industry.

Shared Values Measure-2

ELEMENT	APPLICATION
Diversity Measure	**Number of Times Diversity Values Mentioned as a Strategy to Accomplish the Organization's Business Objectives**
Measure Description	This is a "soft" measure to gauge whether the diversity values are being supported and "shared" in executive presentations.
Suggested Use/Purpose	To unite the organization's employees in valuing and managing diversity to support its strategic business objectives. Specific organizational communications vehicles (such as quarterly newsletters, key speeches, key publications) can be identified in advance to convey these values. Accomplishment targets by week or quarter can be listed.

ELEMENT	APPLICATION
Formula	There is no formula for this measure. The organizational entity responsible for monitoring the organization's commitment to diversity can periodically scan executive and other communications to employees and other audiences regarding diversity's role in the organization's strategic business approach.

Shared Values Measure-3

ELEMENT	APPLICATION
Diversity Measure	**Percent Diversity Values Training Completed**
Measure Description	This measure gauges to what extent awareness and skills are being trained to support organizational expectations relating to diversity. It is based on the number of employees to be trained and the number of sessions needed to train 100% of the population.
Suggested Use/Purpose	To unite the organization's employees in valuing and managing diversity to support its strategic business objectives.
Formula Elements	%DVTC = (TS/N)*100 Where: • DVTC = diversity values training sessions completed • TS = total session trained (*e.g.*, 4) • N = number sessions to complete (*e.g.*, 12)
Example	DVTC = (4/12)*100 = 33.33 = 33%

ELEMENT	APPLICATION
Note:	The organizational entity responsible for monitoring the organization's commitment to diversity can track the completion of this effort. Formulas and tools shown in the skills dimension of the 9-S Framework can be particularly useful. They will help you assess the learner's understanding and skill in demonstrating behaviors that illustrate diversity values.

Shared Values Measure-4

ELEMENT	APPLICATION
Measure	Survey Rating of Values Installation (Actual Number or Percent Rating)
Measure Description	This measure reflects the perception of employees regarding whether diversity values have been woven into the fabric of the organization.
Suggested Use/Purpose	To examine perceptions on key aspects of managerial and employee behavior by measuring the shared values dimension of the Diversity 9-S Framework
Additional Analyses	By level (exempt vs. non-exempt or management level), average, mode, median, and diversity groupings (such as race and gender)
Formula Elements	The formula should be based upon the rating system scale used in your employee survey (*e.g.*, 5-point Likert Scale from Strongly Disagree to Strongly Agree, or 1-Poor to 5-Excellent, and so on). Many employee surveys contain questions relating to the diversity climate. These questions generally

ELEMENT	APPLICATION

assess the employee's perception regarding diversity issues, including how well diversity values and related behaviors have been instilled in the organization's culture.

Typically, the impact of diversity values can be assessed based on the following four categories:

☑ **Knowledge of the Values**: This includes examining ratings on survey questions pertaining to knowledge that a diversity values statement exists. For example, this includes setting rating targets for questions such as "Our organization's stance on the value of diversity is communicated regularly," or "Management's behavior reflects the standards set in our diversity values statement."

☑ **Understanding**: This includes examining ratings on survey questions regarding knowledge of stereotypes, bias, and awareness of and empathy for diverse work group issues. For example, this includes setting rating targets for such questions as, "Employees take care not to make statements that reinforce prejudice or bias in the workplace," or, "It is difficult for new employees to feel a part of the work group," or, "Management should show greater sensitivity to those who are different."

☑ **Acceptance**: This includes examining ratings on questions regarding open-mindedness and respect for diverse work group issues. For example, this includes setting rating targets for such questions as, "It is easier to accept another person's behavior when you know about his/her culture," or "I am comfortable

ELEMENT	APPLICATION
	working with gays, lesbians and bisexuals," or, "In the workplace, people of color earn their position."
	☑ **Behavior**: This includes asking questions to assess whether employees are self-aware and possess interpersonal skills to interact and work with their diverse work group colleagues. For example, this includes setting rating targets for questions such as "Employees tactfully let others know how they feel when they are offended by something that person says or does," or, "Employees adapt their style in order to work effectively with those who are different from themselves," or, "Employees in this organization are aware of how their values and beliefs impact their relationship with others."
Key Analysis or Processing Questions to Examine for this Measure	1. How does it compare with last year's survey rating? Over the last three years? Why? 2. Is the trend going down, up, staying the same? Why? 3. How does this trend or figure compare with others in our industry? Our competition? 4. What are the business implications and consequences of this number based upon the organization's strategic objectives? 5. How does this number compare with best practices standards for this type of data? 6. What should our next steps be in light of this information? Why? When? Who? How? What barriers exist?

Analyzing the Diversity Standards Dimension

THE FOLLOWING INFORMATION PROVIDES AN OVERVIEW of the measures that can be used to monitor the diversity standards dimension.

The standards dimension usually contains a core set of measures that consist of a summary of selected Diversity 9-S Framework measures that exist in your measurement system. It also includes traditional key performance measures (*e.g.*, return on investment (ROI), gross revenue, asset turnover ratio, and so on, depending on your organization's industry). These measures allow you to create a family of measures upon which you can benchmark your overall diversity performance within your organization and industry.

The purpose of the diversity standards dimension is to provide a snapshot that shows how well the organization is doing in critical areas important to the success of an inclusive, diverse work environment. By examining the family of measures that make up this dimension, you should be able to track key changes in your diversity change process.

In chapter four, I covered the Family of Measures method that can assist you in formalizing your standard diversity measures. Simply follow the step-by-step process for creating the Family of Measures Objectives Matrix and select the Diversity 9-S Framework measures as well as performance measures appropriate to your industry. A sample Family of Measures Objectives Matrix is shown on the next page.

FAMILY OF MEASURES METHOD						
Productivity Criteria		Promotion-Ready Minority Employees by Level	Survival/ Loss Rate of New Hires	Termination Rate/Lack of Career Opportunity	Females and Minorities Hired vs. Applicant Flow	Etc
Performance		33	71	20	30	
Target Value	10	49	94	5	55	
	9	45	89	8	49	
	8	41	83	11	45	
	7	37	77	14	41	
	6	33	71	17	37	
Values	5	29	66	19	33	
	4	25	61	21	29	
Base Value	3	21	56	23	25	
	2	17	51	25	21	
	1	13	46	27	17	
	0	10	41	29	13	
Score		6.0	6.0	4.8	4.2	
Weight		40	30	15	15	
Value		240	180	72	63	
INDEX:		555 *				

This core group of measures might cover such aspects as:

• Productivity

• Quality

• Utilization

• Creativity or innovation

• Outcomes

• Financial performance

Though the Family of Measures method may take a bit more time, it is an excellent way to provide an aggregate and motivational evaluation of your organization's diversity initiatives. By evaluating how well the organization is doing across this wide range of indices, you can judge the effectiveness of the diversity change process.

It is also important to use diversity standard measures as benchmarks throughout your organization, with competitors, and within your industry. The benchmarking process entails completing the following steps:

STEP	WHAT'S INCLUDED
1. Identify What to Benchmark	☑ Clarify the benchmarking objective ☑ Decide whom to involve ☑ Define the process that the diversity metric measures ☑ Consider the scope ☑ Set the boundaries ☑ Agree on what happens in the process ☑ Flow chart the process the diversity metric is measuring
2. Determine What to Measure	☑ Examine the flow chart ☑ Review the process for additional measures that may be calculated ☑ Verify that the measures match objectives
3. Identify Who to Benchmark	☑ Conduct general research on organizations and their diversity programs ☑ Choose level to benchmark: internal, competitive, non-competitive, world-class

STEP	WHAT'S INCLUDED
4. Collect the Data	☑ Use a questionnaire or consistent format for analysis and summary ☑ Conduct a benchmark site visit (as appropriate)
5. Analyze Data and Determine the Gap	☑ Quantitative data analysis ☑ Qualitative data analysis
6. Set Goals and Develop an Action Plan	☑ Set performance goals ☑ Develop an action plan
7. Monitor the process	☑ Track the changes ☑ Make benchmarking a habit

The diversity shared vision, shared values, and standards dimensions of the Diversity 9-S Framework provide critical foundation metrics for tracking diversity initiatives. In the next chapter, we will continue this examination by exploring measures that support the structure, strategy and systems dimensions.

CHAPTER 7 Diversity Strategy, Structure, and Systems: Establishing Tactical, Organizational Form, and Policy Measures

INTRODUCTION

DIVERSITY ACTIVITIES CAN IMPACT VIRTUALLY EVERY ASPECT of organizational life. If an organization wants to manage diversity according to shared vision, shared values, and standards, it is necessary to change organizational processes, systems, and employee behavior.

There are a number of basic levers or forces that can be used to influence operational, cultural, and employee behavioral changes. Some are more important than others, but principally the levers include the following:

- Strategy

- Structure

- Systems

- Skills

- Staff

- Style

By developing measures and monitoring changes in all Diversity 9-S Framework dimensions, the vision of a more inclusive work environment has an improved chance for success.

In this chapter, we will examine measures covering the diversity strategy, structure, and systems dimension of the Diversity 9-S Framework.

MEASURES THAT SUPPORT DIVERSITY STRATEGY, STRUCTURE, AND SYSTEMS

THE FOLLOWING DIVERSITY MEASURES WILL BE DISCUSSED in this chapter (they are not intended to be exhaustive, but they do reflect some possible measures to use in each area):

Strategy Measures

1. *Writing the diversity business rationale strategy*

2. *Number of times diversity business rationale mentioned as a strategy to accomplish the organization's business objectives.*

3. *Percentage of diversity goals attained (overall or by group)*

4. *Number of diversity goals completed by department*

5. *Number of diversity goals assigned by department*

Structure Measures

1. *Degree of variation by diversity dimension*

2. *Number of diverse work teams by strategic result area*

3. *Number of departmental or divisional differences represented on a team*

4. *Number of management levels represented on a team*

5. *Number of geographical differences represented on a team*

Systems Measures

1. *Diversity tied to management compensation*

2. *Average hourly rate*

3. *Absence rate*

4. *Absenteeism cost*

5. *Effect of absenteeism on labor utilization*

6. *Percentage gender-based pay differential*

7. *Number and type of policies and procedures assessed for diverse workforce impact*

8. *Number and type of policies and procedures changed to support diversity*

9. *Diversity performance appraisal metrics*

Now, let's explore the measures that support the diversity strategy, structure, and systems dimension of the Diversity 9-S Framework.

ANALYZING THE DIVERSITY STRATEGY DIMENSION

THE FOLLOWING INFORMATION PROVIDES AN OVERVIEW of the diversity measures and associated formulas that can be used to monitor the diversity strategy dimension.

The diversity strategy dimension clarifies the tactics and practices needed to transform the organization into a more inclusive, diverse workplace. These tactics and practices include:

- Leadership and management accountability to create ownership and involvement at all levels

- Establishing a diversity performance evaluation system tied to compensation

- Staffing and recruiting approaches

- Internship programs for nontraditional employees (high school, college, trade school, professional skill

- Creating work/life balance alternatives

- Revising career development and succession planning systems

- Matching customer demographics with employee demographics for products and services

One task that is essential to communicating the organization's approach is the diversity business rationale statement. Adapted from the business rationale example created by Larry Baytos, it summarizes the business reasons and tactics the organization will use to build an organization consistent with the shared diversity vision and values.

The wording and communication media appropriate to your organization will depend upon the nature of the products or services being provided, the culture of the organization, the types of jobs and educational level of the workforce, and related factors. You may need to vary the emphasis of the statement depending on the internal and external audiences covered.

> You may want to keep in mind the following guidelines while you prepare and communicate your diversity business rationale:

- While your full statement may be lengthy for senior management purposes, a condensed version is more appropriate for communicating to target audiences.

- Don't include too many factors or the explanation may lose clarity and power.

- Use many examples that are relevant to your own organization.

- Minimize jargon and technical terms.

- Relate the conditions and issues the organization now faces to those previously encountered. Identify the cost of not addressing the issues.

- Don't beat around the bush. If you are "doing diversity" to keep your government contracts, admit it.

Now let's take a look at a sample diversity business rationale for a hypothetical organization, Trans-National, Inc.:

SAMPLE BUSINESS RATIONALE FOR DIVERSITY INITIATIVES
TRANS-NATIONAL, INC.

Background

The Management Committee of Trans-National, Inc. (TNI) has completed a preliminary review of issues that should be addressed with regard to meeting the needs and fully utilizing the abilities of our diverse workforce. We have concluded that our Succeeding Through Diversity effort will be a principal priority for the company for the following reasons:

Marketing and Sales Opportunities

The strong base of consumers of TNI's products historically has been White males in our core Midwestern markets. However, future growth will come from outside this historical base, and we must recognize these realities:

- We will be entering markets in the South and Southwest that have heavy concentrations of Hispanic consumers. We have little experience in targeting such markets.
- Our market share among Black consumers is only 4% versus our 6% share of White consumers.
- Females currently make the purchasing decisions for 18% of total "XXX" sales and 65% of other sales. However, our marketing approach has not been effective with female consumers.
- Chain store buyers who make decisions about whether or not to stock or distribute our products are becoming increasingly diverse. We no longer look like our customers, and there may be some effect on results if we don't address the issue.

The continued growth and profitability of the company is dependent upon maintaining our positions in core geographic and demographic segments, while improving our success in the

SAMPLE BUSINESS RATIONALE FOR DIVERSITY INITIATIVES
TRANS-NATIONAL, INC.

areas listed above. To achieve that success, we must have a work-force and management team who reflect the changing marketplace and who can understand and respond to the needs of the changing consumer. We must also reassess our community relations pro-grams, corporate contribution programs, and purchasing from minority and women-owned enterprises so that we target the total resources of the company toward the pursuit of this goal.

Recruitment and Retention

As stated in our corporate objectives, we intend to be a world-class employer, utilizing to the fullest the skills and talents of our entire workforce. However, we are aware that the culture, the systems or the programs have not been equally effective for all employees. For example:

- Overall voluntary separations increased from 8% to 12% during the past two years. We have lost a lot of good talent.
- The turnover rate for minority employees increased from 10% to 16% during that same time period.
- Turnover for female employees is at 16%. About 40% of our female employees do not return to work after delivering their first child. Many report through exit interview data that our company makes few allowances for work and family issues, particularly situations around flexible workplaces and hours.
- Our extensive affirmative action efforts have succeeded in recruiting a diverse workforce. However, we have been relatively unsuccessful in promoting females and minorities to the director or officer level.

The issues described above have a tremendous bottom-line impact in recruitment, training, and productivity costs. We can neither consider ourselves a world-class employer nor sustain our continued growth and success unless we create an environment that values and fully utilizes all employees.

Strategy Measure-1

ELEMENT	APPLICATION
Diversity Measure	**Writing the Diversity Business Rationale**
Measure Description	This measure benchmarks whether the organization has invested the time and effort to craft a diversity business rationale statement.
Suggested Use/Purpose	To explain the organization's business reasons and tactics to value and manage diversity initiatives in support of its strategic business objectives. The completion of this task should be listed as a milestone within the strategic business plan.
Formula	There is no formula other than the presence or absence of the diversity business rationale. However, this task should be listed as a milestone in the strategic plan with input and participation from members of the organization. A representative body (a diversity steering committee or diversity advisory board) with a cross-section of the employee base can serve as a resource to help formulate a draft and the final business rationale document.

Strategy Measure-2

ELEMENT	APPLICATION
Diversity Measure	**Number of Times Diversity Business Rationale Mentioned as a Strategy to Accomplish the Organization's Business Objectives.**

ELEMENT	APPLICATION
Measure Description	This is a "soft" measure to gauge whether the diversity business rationale is being supported and shared in executive presentations.
Suggested Use/Purpose	To increase the organization's understanding of the business reasons for valuing and managing diversity
Formula	There is no formula for this measure. The organizational entity responsible for monitoring the organization's commitment to diversity can periodically scan executive and other communications to employees and other audiences regarding diversity's role in the organization's strategic business approach.

Strategy Measure-3

ELEMENT	APPLICATION
Diversity Measure	**Percentage of Diversity Goals Completed**
Measure Description	This measure is designed to gauge (against the organization's plan) the percentage of diversity initiatives that are completed. It serves as instant feedback at a gross level to report the level of progress being made.
Suggested Use/Purpose	To quantify the progress and movement towards an inclusive, diverse work environment Other analyses that are useful to this form of tracking include: • Number of diversity goals completed by department • Number of diversity goals assigned by department

ELEMENT	APPLICATION
Formula Elements	**%DGC** = (total number goals completed /total number diversity goals)* 100 Where: • %DGC = percentage of diversity goals completed • TNGC = total number of diversity goals completed (*e.g.*, 22) • TDG = total diversity goals (*e.g.*, 57)
Example	%DGC = (22/57)*100 = (.3859) x 100 = 38.6%
Key Analysis or Processing Questions to Examine for this Measure	1. Is the percentage acceptable? 2. Is it on target with the planned diversity change effort? 3. How does this percentage compare by department, division, or region? 4. How does this figure compare with others in our industry? Our competition? 5. What are the business implications and consequences of this number based upon the organization's strategic objectives? 6. How does this number compare with best practices standards for this type of data and the number of weeks or months we have been working on these objectives? 7. What should our next steps be in light of this information? Why? When? Who? How? What barriers exist?

ANALYZING THE DIVERSITY STRUCTURE DIMENSION

THE FOLLOWING INFORMATION PROVIDES AN OVERVIEW of the diversity measures and associated formulas that can be used to monitor the diversity structure dimension of the organization.

Each dimension of diversity contributes to the organization's identity and view of the world. It is vitally important to assess the impact of diversity on the organization. To gain a better understanding of your diverse personnel structure, the following exercise (adapted from Gardenswartz and Rowe) will be helpful. Simply follow the directions below and complete both ratings (1-5 and + or -):

Structure Measure-1

Directions: Think about each dimension of diversity and rate the degree of variation in the organization by checking the appropriate column. Put a "+" in the last column, if you feel the degree of difference is put to good use by the organization; put a "-" there if it is not well used or if more diversity is needed to move the organization forward.

DEGREE OF VARIATION						
	1	2	3	4	5	+ or -
	Little Difference				Great Deal of Difference	
Personality						
Different Styles and Characteristics						
Internal Dimensions						
Age						
Gender						
Sexual Orientation						
Physical Ability						
Ethnicity						
Race						

	DEGREE OF VARIATION					
	1	2	3	4	5	+ or -
	Little Difference				Great Deal of Difference	
External Dimensions						
Geographic Location						
Income						
Personal Habits						
Recreational Habits						
Religion						
Education						
Work Experience						
Appearance						
Parental Status						
Marital Status						
Organizational Dimensions						
Functional Level / Classification						
Work Content / Field						
Division / Department / Unit / Group						
Seniority						
Work Location						
Union Affiliation						
Management Status						

This chart can be used for analyzing teams as well as an organization. For example, if all have the same level and type of education, they would rate that factor 1 (low diversity). If team members come from 10 different countries or nationalities and speak many different languages, the team might rate a 5 (high diversity) on the ethnicity dimension.

Once the rating has been completed, the team can discuss what difference the presence or lack of diversity makes for the team or the organization. Teams can also discuss which dimensions seem to be the most critical in terms of teamwork.

Another approach is to identify the top three dimensions that seem to make the greatest difference on the team or in the organization. It is also important to discuss how these differences are demonstrated and how they affect teamwork, productivity, and the organization's inclusive, diverse workforce strategy. Be sure to focus on both the pluses and minuses and the importance of managing both.

Structure Measure-2

ELEMENT	APPLICATION
Diversity Measure	**Number of Diverse Work Teams by Strategic Result Area**
Measure Description	This measure allows you to track the number of diverse work teams operating in the organization that are assigned to critical strategic result areas related to the business plan. This assumes that customer and organizational needs have been matched with diverse talents and backgrounds that exist in the organization.
Suggested Use/Purpose	To track workforce utilization. Other analyses that are useful to this form of tracking include: • *Number of departmental or divisional differences represented on a team* • *Number of management levels represented on a*

ELEMENT	APPLICATION
	team • *Number of geographical differences represented on a team*
Formula	There is no formula other than a matrix to monitor the number of diverse work teams. You can also use the Degree of Variation by Diversity Dimension Matrix in conjunction with this tracking tool to assess the specific diversity represented by the team. A modified version of the tool is shown following this section.
Sample Format	*Number of Teams* *Strategic Results Area* 3 Analyze the need for on-site daycare 1 Conduct diversity values training

Structure Measure-3

Directions: Think about each dimension of diversity represented on the team working in a strategic result area and place an "x" in the appropriate row. Put a "+" in the last column, if you feel the degree of difference is put to good use in this team; put a "-" there if it is not well used or if better utilization is needed to move the organization forward.

DEGREE OF VARIATION		
	Present in Team	+ or -
Personality		
Different Styles and Characteristics		
Internal Dimensions		
Age		
Gender		
Sexual Orientation		
Physical Ability		
Ethnicity		
Race		
External Dimensions		
Geographic Location		
Income		
Personal Habits		
Recreational Habits		
Religion		
Education		
Work Experience		
Appearance		
Parental Status		
Marital Status		
Organizational Dimensions		
Functional Level / Classification		
Work Content / Field		
Division / Department / Unit / Group		
Seniority		
Work Location		
Union Affiliation		
Management Status		

Analyzing the Diversity Systems Dimension

THE FOLLOWING INFORMATION PROVIDES AN OVERVIEW of the diversity measures and associated formulas that can be used to monitor the diversity systems dimension.

Systems dimension measures allow you to examine whether policies, procedures, systems, regulations, structure, and rules support or are in conflict with diversity initiatives. The first place to start looking for measures is in what already is being measured that could impact diversity initiatives. This examination can allow the organization to adjust and expand into diversity systems naturally.

One systems method for implementing the goal of management and/or employee accountability is to create a diversity incentive system that is developmental. The following example illustrates a five-year transition system for installing accountability for diversity initiatives.

Systems Measure-1

Year	Activity-Based Measures	Results-Based Measures
Bonus Percentages by Period:	Requires managers to attend courses on diversity and to be active in diverse and/or multi-cultural workforce activities and events.	Involves meeting the qualitative and quantitative metrics, ratios, and goals for hiring rates, training, promotion, succession planning, and other developments of staff.
	Requirements:	Requirements:
Year 1	100% of Bonus Percentage	0% of Bonus Percentage
Year 2	75%	25%
Year 3	50%	50%
Year 4	25%	75%
Year 5	0%	100%

Note: This accountability system is developmental. Rewards can be given through informal or formal channels (depending on the culture), resulting in higher visibility and more incentives for those who participate actively in diversity.

This system illustrates how a supervisory and management accountability system can be created to transition the organization toward performance and incentive-based diversity metrics. It shows that as time passes, managers and supervisors gain increasing responsibility for diversity results rather than completing diversity activities. This should not suggest that organizations focus only on results. It is also important to examine the process by which the results are attained. Activity-based measures help build awareness and lay the foundation for accepting responsibility for results.

Systems Measure-2

ELEMENT	APPLICATION
Measure	**Average Hourly Rate**
Measure Description	The basic calculation that computes an average hourly rate for employees
Suggested Use/Purpose	This calculation is useful when computing other measures that rely directly or indirectly on an employee wage average.
Formula Elements	$$R/h = \frac{P}{EHW}$$ Where: • R/h = average hourly wage or salary paid • P = total wages and salaries paid (*e.g.*, \$57,017,000) • EHW = Total annual employee hours worked times number of employees (*e.g.*, 2,080 x 1,400)

ELEMENT	APPLICATION
Example	$$R/h = \frac{\$57,017,000}{2,080 \times 1,400}$$ $$= \frac{\$57,017,000}{2,912,000}$$ $$= \quad \$19.51$$ By adding the hours worked variable to the gross productivity calculation (reviewed in chapter 6) you have refined a gross compensation number into an hourly one. This is more workable. It is difficult for a person to deal with an 8-digit number. The figure \$57,017,000 is useful to rally support for an efficiency or productivity drive, but \$19.51 is a human-scale number. Employees can say, "If our diverse work team can find a way to save just 10 cents an hour in labor cost, that will save the organization almost \$300,000!"
Key Analysis or Processing Questions to Examine for this Measure	1. What are the reasons that support this figure? 2. How does this rate compare with this same period last year, last month, Over the last three years? Why? 3. Is the trend going down, up, staying the same? Why? 4. How does this trend or figure compare with others in our industry? Our competition? 5. What are the business implications and consequences of this number based upon the organization's strategic objectives? 6. How does this number compare with best practices standards for this type of data? 7. What should our next steps be in light of this information? Why? When? Who? How? What barriers exist?

ELEMENT	APPLICATION
Possible Graphic	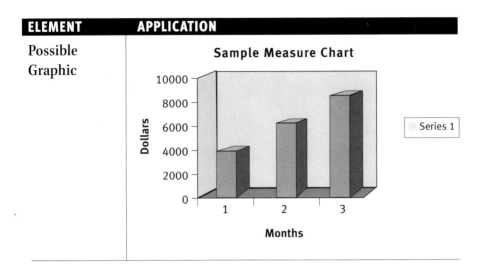

Systems Measure-3

Absence Rate

Employee absence occurs in organizations for many reasons. Survey data often show a correlation between absence and dissatisfaction. Various sources of irritation and stress can prompt an absence. Poor supervisory practices most often correlate with turnover, but they may also foster absence. Poor interpersonal, non-inclusive environments can have a tremendous effect on employee morale and productivity. At times, to put themselves in a better mood or to escape, absence is used as a way of coping with high levels of stress.

In the Gold Study, conducted by Ann Morrison and others, many employees reported what this stress is like on a day-to-day basis when differences are perceived as weaknesses due to prejudice. They stated they are made to feel:

☐ They can't make mistakes

☐ They can't say no

☐ Isolated ("Too few like myself who can relate to what I am going through")

☐ Co-worker hostility ("Withholding of information," "side step-ping," "going around me," "exclusion")

☐ They're "tapped to serve on every task force to bring the '_____' perspective (in a token way)

☐ "Someone is raising the bar while I am still in the air."

☐ Over-scrutinized on their performance

☐ An imbalance of challenge, recognition, and support

With this type of daily stress, absenteeism provides a periodic safe haven for relief. Whatever the cause, there are several ways to measure the absence rate of occurrence and its cost to the organization.

The basic absence rate calculation used in most national surveys follows. It can be used as a systemic measure to track absenteeism by diverse work group category as an indicator for further study to identify why it is occurring.

ELEMENT	APPLICATION
Measure	Absence Rate
Measure Description	The rate at which worker days are lost through absence

ELEMENT	APPLICATION
Suggested Use/Purpose	To gain an indication of potential employee issues that may be caused by a poor diversity climate
Additional Analyses	As with most other ratios, this one can be computed by diversity dimension and department to find locations where absence levels are relatively high. It can also be applied to job groups to gauge if particular groups are impacted.
Formula Elements	$$AR = \frac{WDL}{e \times WD}$$ Where: • AR = absence rate • WDL = worker days lost through absence (*e.g.*, 400) • e = average employee population (*e.g.*, 550) • WD = number of work days available per employee (*e.g.*, 22)
Example	$$AR = \frac{400}{550 \times 22}$$ $$= \frac{400}{12,100}$$ $$= \quad 3.3\%$$
Key Analysis or Processing Questions to Examine for this Measure	1. What are the reasons that support this figure? 2. How does this rate compare with this same period last year, last month, Over the last three years? Why? 3. Is the trend going down, up, staying the same? Why? 4. How does this trend or figure compare with others in our industry? Our competition? 5. What are the business implications and consequences of this number based upon the organization's strategic objectives?

ELEMENT	APPLICATION
	6. How does this number compare with best practices standards for this type of data? 7. What should our next steps be in light of this information? Why? When? Who? How? What barriers exist?
Possible Graphic	**Sample Measure Chart** (bar chart: Percent vs Months; bars at 1≈3, 2≈6, 3≈9; Series 1)

Systems Measure-4

ELEMENT	APPLICATION
Measure	Absenteeism Cost
Measure Description	Knowing the amount of time lost through absence is only the starting point. The other issue is the hidden cost of absence.
Suggested Use/Purpose	To calculate the cost of time lost due to absenteeism that may be linked to diversity-related causes. It provides an understanding of the financial impact of this behavior.

ELEMENT	APPLICATION
Additional Analyses	As with most other ratios, this one can be computed by diversity dimension and department to find locations where absence levels are relatively high. It can also be applied to job groups to gauge whether particular groups are impacted.
Formula Elements	$$AC/E = \frac{ML(Wh+EBC)+S(R/h+SBC)+MISC}{E}$$ Where: • AC/E = absence cost per employee • ML = total work hours lost for all reasons except holidays and vacations (*e.g.*, 78,336) • Wh = weighted average hourly pay level for groups (*e.g.*, 85% of hourly absences at $6.25 = $5.31; 13% of non-exempt absences at $5.95 = $0.77; 2% of exempt absences at $12.45 = $0.25; total $6.33) • EBC = cost of employee benefits (*e.g.*, 35% of pay: $6.33 x 35% = $2.22) • S = supervisory hours lost due to employee absence, based on sampling to estimate average hours per day spent dealing with problems resulting from absences: production rescheduling, instructing replacements, counseling and disciplining absentees (*e.g.*, ½ hour per day = 3,840) • R/h = average hourly pay for supervisors (*e.g.*, $7.25) • SBC = cost of supervisor's benefits (*e.g.*, 35% of $7.25 = $2.54) • Misc = other costs, temporary help, overtime, production losses, machine downtime, quality problems (*e.g.*, $38,500) • E = total employees (*e.g.*, 1,200)

ELEMENT	APPLICATION
Example	$$AC/E = \frac{(78,336 \times \$8.55)+(3840 \times \$9.79)+\$38,500}{1,200}$$ $$= \frac{\$669,773+\$37,954+\$38,500}{1,200}$$ $$= \frac{\$745,867}{1,200}$$ $$= \$621.56$$
Key Analysis or Processing Questions to Examine for this Measure	1. What is the cost per year per employee? 2. What is the total cost based upon each critical diversity segment? 3. How does it compare with this same period last year, last month, Over the last three years? Why? 4. Is the trend going down, up, staying the same? Why? 5. How does this trend or figure compare with others in our industry? Our competition? 6. What are the business implications and consequences of this number based upon the organization's strategic objectives? 7. How does this number compare with best practices standards for this type of data? 8. What should our next steps be in light of this information? Why? When? Who? How? What barriers exist?
Possible Graphic	**Sample Measure Chart** *(bar chart: Dollars from 0 to 10000 on y-axis, Month 1, 2, 3 on x-axis; Series 1)*

Measuring this quantity brings home to the organization that absence carries with it a high hidden cost. The peripheral costs of supervisory time, temporary help, and poor quality work add significantly to the loss. Significant reductions in absenteeism can quickly add up to thousands or millions of dollars saved in pay for time not worked.

Another way of viewing absence is from the standpoint of its effect on labor utilization. This is accomplished using a two-step process:

Systems Measure-5

ELEMENT	APPLICATION
Measure	**Effect of Absenteeism on Labor Utilization**
Measure Description	The impact absence can have on the rate at which personnel is effectively utilized. If the diversity climate has in any way contributed to an employee taking the day off, labor utilization rates for the organization will be affected.
Suggested Use/Purpose	To gain insight into the impact that absence caused by a poor diversity climate can have on a organization
Additional Analyses	As with most other measures, this one can be computed by diversity dimension and department to find locations where labor utilization levels are lower due to absenteeism. It can also be applied to job groups to gauge if particular groups are adversely impacted more than others.

ELEMENT	APPLICATION
Formula Elements	$U = \dfrac{Nh}{h}$ Where: · U = labor utilization percentage · Nh = nonproductive hours: absence, breaks, downtime, prep time, rework (*e.g.*, 380) · h = work hours available (*e.g.*, 10 employees x 40 hours x 4 weeks = 1600 hours)
Example	**Step 1:** $$U = \frac{380}{1,600}$$ $= \;\; 24\% \quad$ *(utilization = 76%)* ***Step 2:*** *To show the effect of absenteeism, subtract the absent hours due to diversity climate issues (e.g., 80 hours) from Nh and re-compute as shown below:* $$U = \frac{380 - 80}{1,600}$$ $= \;\; 19\% \quad$ *(utilization = 81%)* Based upon this calculation, utilization would have been 5% higher if no employees had been absent for this reason. In today's marketplace, that could contribute significantly to competitive advantage. Absence is a slow-death type of problem because it is, by definition, invisible. It is not so obviously a matter of something going wrong as it is something that should occur not occurring. The missing occurrence is the arrival of the scheduled employee at work. When that does not happen, it sets in motion a chain of other events that negatively impact hard measures such as quality and productivity as well as human stress imposed on other employees by the absence.

ELEMENT	APPLICATION
Key Analysis or Processing Questions to Examine for this Measure	1. What is the lost utilization percentage? 2. What are the reasons that support this figure that are clearly diversity issues? 3. How does this rate compare with this same period last year, last month, Over the last three years? Why? 4. Is the trend going down, up, staying the same? Why? 5. How does this trend or figure compare with others in our industry? Our competition? 6. What are the business implications and consequences of this number based upon the organization's strategic objectives? 7. What should our next steps be in light of this information? Why? When? Who? How? What barriers exist?
Possible Graphic	**Sample Measure Chart** Percent / Months chart with Series 1

Systems Measure-6

ELEMENT	APPLICATION
Measure	**Percentage of Gender-Based Pay Differential**
Measure Description	This measure helps to identify if there are pay differences that exist by gender.
Suggested Use/Purpose	To gain insight into historical pay rates by gender. This measure helps the organization gauge whether inequalities in pay exist and provides a foundation on which to correct the problem.
Additional Analyses	This measure displays salary differences on a gross salary basis. As with most other measures, this one can be computed by diversity dimension and department to find locations where gender-based pay differential exists to set priorities and goals for correction. For example, some jobs or locations may have a disproportionate share of these differences and may warrant a higher priority.
Formula Elements	$$GBPD = \frac{TSBG}{TS}$$ Where: • GBPD = gender-based pay differential percentage • TSBG = total salaries paid by gender (*e.g.*, \$880,000 to males, \$290,000 to females) • TS = total salaries paid (*e.g.*, \$1,170,000)
Example	$$GBPD = \frac{\$880,000}{\$1,170,000}$$ = 75.2% for males $$GBPD = \frac{\$290,000}{\$1,170,000}$$ = 24.8% females Difference: 75.2% - 24.8% = 50.4%

ELEMENT	APPLICATION
Key Analysis or Processing Questions to Examine for this Measure	1. What is the gender-based pay differential percentage? 2. How does this percentage compare with this same period last year, last month, Over the last three years? Why? 3. Is the trend going down, up, staying the same? Why? 4. How does this trend or figure compare with others in our industry? Our competition? 5. What are the business implications and consequences of this number based upon the organization's strategic objectives? 6. What should our next steps be in light of this information? Why? When? Who? How? What barriers exist?
Possible Graphic	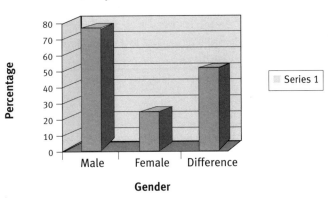 Sample Measure Chart

Systems Measure-7

ELEMENT	APPLICATION
Diversity Measure(s)	• *Number and type of policies and procedures assessed for diverse workforce impact* • *Number and type of policies and procedures changed to support diversity*
Measure Description	These are "soft" measures to gauge whether policies and procedures have been examined and changed to support a more diversity-friendly climate.
Suggested Use/Purpose	These measures help you monitor specific actions taken and changes made to strategically align organizational operations with diversity initiatives.
Formula	There is no formula for this measure. The organizational entity responsible for monitoring the organization's commitment to diversity can periodically scan policies to assess their consistency with diversity initiatives. In addition, the following form can be used for tracking purposes.

Policy Tracking Worksheet

Number	Policy / Procedure	Diversity Impact	Status: Change No-Change Pending C, NC, P	Comments
2.1.1	Divisional Succession Planning	In the past, this policy has been based upon talent pools that existed in our current divisional operations without regard to changing market demographics. In the future, we must assess changing customer and employee statistics to assess our compatibility with the markets we serve.	C	This policy is slated for the September strategic business conference for all divisions. A diverse, cross-functional task force is being convened to assess and report on specific data and plans by division at this meeting.

Systems Measure-8

ELEMENT	APPLICATION
Measure	**Percentage of Diversity Turnover by Performance Level**
Measure Description	This measure reflects the amount of diverse workforce turnover experienced by the department or organization.
Suggested Use/Purpose	It is often enlightening to look at systems measures that track turnover from more than one perspective at a time. For example, you could correlate diversity turnover data by age and level of performance. First, you could compute the percentage of turnover for age groups (e.g., 20 to 25, 26 to 30, 31 to 35, and so on). Then you could do the

ELEMENT	APPLICATION
	same for levels of performance. The formulas shown in this section illustrate the method.
Formula Elements	$$DPT = \frac{R}{L} \qquad DPT = \frac{R}{TR}$$ Where: • DPT = percent diversity employees terminating at each performance level • R = number rated at each level • L = total number terminated • TR = total rated at a given level
Example	$DPT = \frac{27}{225} = 12.0\%$ or $DPT = \frac{27}{79} = 34.2\%$ LVL 6 $DPT = \frac{79}{225} = 35.1\%$ or $DPT = \frac{79}{365} = 21.6\%$ LVL 5 $DPT = \frac{63}{225} = 20.0\%$ or $DPT = \frac{63}{593} = 10.6\%$ LVL 4 $DPT = \frac{42}{225} = 18.7\%$ or $DPT = \frac{42}{53} = 79.2\%$ LVL 3 $DPT = \frac{8}{225^*} = 3.6\%$ or $DPT = \frac{8}{10^*} = 80.0\%$ LVL 2 * Column adds to 219 + 6 who did not get rated. These statistics (based upon a 6-level performance appraisal structure) suggest the following: In the employee sample, 225 diverse work group employees were terminated. Twenty-seven were rated 6, or the highest level in their performance. In the total organization, 79 were rated 6. This means that while 12 percent of the terminations came from Level 6, these diverse work group employees represented 34.2 percent of the organization's highest performers leaving to work somewhere else!

ELEMENT	APPLICATION
Key Analysis or Processing Questions to	1. How do these percentages compare with this same period last year, last month, Over the last three years? Why? 2. Is the trend going down, up, staying the same? Why? 3. How does this trend compare with others in our industry? Our competition? 4. What are the business implications and consequences of this number based upon the organization's strategic objectives? 5. What should our next steps be in light of this information? Why? When? Who? How? What barriers exist?
Possible Graphic	**Sample Measure Chart for LVL 6** Percent (y-axis: 0, 10, 20, 30, 40, 50) — Months (x-axis: 1, 2, 3) — Series 1

An additional measure that can be obtained is the performance level of the terminee. This can be obtained through a weighted average calculation of the left column. The answer in this sample is 4.27. In order to correlate age, performance, and turnover you need both the age and performance rating of each terminee.

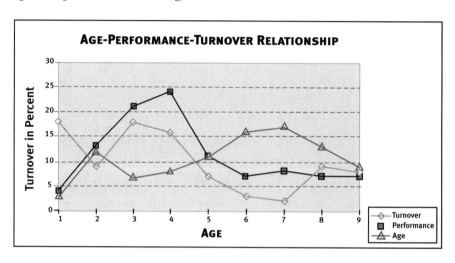

Age-Range Legend:

1 = 20 - 24	4 = 35 - 39	7 = 50 - 54
2 = 25 - 29	5 = 40 - 44	8 = 55 - 59
3 = 30 - 34	6 = 45 - 49	9 = 60 - 65

When you have the three types of data you can plot them on a line chart. In the sample chart above, we are interested only in high performers. They are defined here as employees with 5 or 6 ratings on the 6-point scale. Employees with ratings of 1 to 4 are not included.

This example shows an organization with some problems. You can no doubt see that turnover is highest from about age 25 to 39, which is also the age group that has a large percentage of high performers. In addition, as age increases the percent who are high performers decreases. The profile shows a very large group in the 45 to 54 range. This last observation alone is worth further study for questions such as potential age discrimination, lack of skill development opportunity for this age group, which may have impacted performance, or, simply, poor performance. If you put some of these findings together you can see that there is reason for concern across all three dimensions. Multidimensional analysis is the best way to get inside the numbers to find correlations that point to otherwise invisible organizational issues.

The measures presented here are a small sampling of the variety of diversity systems measures that can be used. The diversity systems dimension offers diversity professionals an excellent organizational arena where analytic and creative skills can be used to obtain visible results. Because the elements of this dimension are very quantifiable, you will be able to demonstrate to management exactly how this aspect of the diversity change process contributes to the bottom-line.

CHAPTER 8 Diversity Skills: Creating Training Evaluation Measures

INTRODUCTION

SKILL DEVELOPMENT IS ONE OF SEVERAL ACTIVITIES THAT MUST be undertaken to achieve an organization's strategic diversity objectives. The only way to determine that diversity training and skill development are having the desired effect is to use formal training evaluation processes and cost-benefit analysis methods. The results of these activities can confirm the positive effects of training and development and identify improvements to make it better. Evaluation can contribute to maximizing the organization's return on training investment. This chapter illustrates approaches that can be used to identify "hard" and "soft" training measures for diversity.

EVALUATION

EVALUATION MEANS TO MEASURE SOMETHING IN PREPARATION for making a decision: for example, to stop, modify, or expand it to increase its benefits. This implies:

- Knowing what decision the evaluation data will help you make.

- Measuring scientifically, using data collection methods and research designs that separate the effects your program is having from all other influences on your outcome variables.

• Choosing the right measures for what your program is really trying to accomplish.

Evaluation efforts throughout this book can be described as formative or summative. Formative means evaluation data are used to see how a program is doing, to modify it or improve it. Summative means data are used to make a final judgement on a program: it worked or it didn't, was or was not worth its cost, should be continued or dropped.

TYPES OF SKILL DEVELOPMENT MEASURES

IT IS USEFUL FIRST TO DISTINGUISH RESULTS MEASURES FROM OTHER types of measures commonly used to evaluate human resource programs. In a famous article, Kirkpatrick observed that training and other programs could be evaluated at one of four levels: reaction, learning, behavior, results. Building on this model, Jack Phillips added a fifth level: return on investment. A summary of the model levels is shown below:

KIRKPATRICK SKILLS EVALUATION MODEL PLUS	
Level	**Description**
Level 1: Reaction	How people feel (reactions) about the diversity skill development program and what do they plan to do with the material?
Level 2: Learning	Whether people know anything as a result of the diversity skill development program. What skills, knowledge, or attitudes have changed and by how much?
Level 3: Behavior	Whether people do anything differently after the diversity skill development program. Did participants apply on the job what they learned?

KIRKPATRICK SKILLS EVALUATION MODEL PLUS	
Level	Description
Level 4: *Results*	Hard outcome measures of individual or organizational effectiveness produced by the diversity skills development program. Did the on-the-job application of this program produce measurable results?
Level 5: *Return-on-* *Training* *Investment*	Financial results of the diversity skills development program. Did the monetary value of the results exceed the cost for the program?

Caution! The four levels of evaluation should be used in sequence. It is acceptable to use Levels 1 and 2 by themselves. Levels 3 and 4 should not normally be used unless you have positive results from a Level 2 evaluation. Without a Level 2 evaluation, it is difficult to relate the results of Level 3 evaluation back to training. This is because factors other than training can influence on-the-job transfer. If you do a Level 3 without a Level 2, you need to rule out these other factors before you can assume that training had positive or negative outcomes. With Level 4 evaluation, it is important to have some evidence of training results at both the learning and transfer levels. Once this is accomplished, you can begin to explore the cost-benefit, return-on-investment relationship that ties the Diversity training effort to the bottom-line.

How Much Training Evaluation Do You Need?

ANYONE RESPONSIBLE FOR DIVERSITY TRAINING IS ALSO RESPONSIBLE for evaluation. The amount of evaluation that you provide depends on the types of decisions that your organization must make and the information needed to make those decisions. For example, if your only requirement is to ensure that participants have positive attitudes toward the course, then Level 1 evaluation is sufficient. But, if your goal is to determine whether your diversity course is having a positive effect on job performance, then you will have to do Level 3 evaluation, and this means that you will also have to do Level 1 and 2. They provide the basis for determining whether participants want to use what they have learned and have indeed learned the appropriate attitudes and skills.

WHERE DO YOU BEGIN?

YOUR FIRST STEP IN EVALUATING DIVERSITY TRAINING IS TO determine your major evaluation questions. The second step is to use the relevant sections of this chapter to plan and conduct the appropriate level of training evaluation. The following decision table may help you identify some of the major questions and methods:

MAJOR QUESTIONS	EVALUATION TECHNIQUE
How satisfied are the participants with the course?	**Level 1:** Reaction evaluation
Do the participants believe that they learned the values and skills that the course was intended to teach?	**Level 2:** Learning evaluation. Use the learning self-assessment evaluation tool.
Can the participants demonstrate the values, knowledge, and skills that are taught in the course?	**Level 2:** Learning evaluation. Use the short-answer evaluation tool.
Do the participants report that they are using their diversity values, knowledge, and skills on the job?	**Level 3:** Behavior evaluation. Use the post-training survey for course participants.

MAJOR QUESTIONS	EVALUATION TECHNIQUE
Do the managers of the participants have the impression that the participants are using their diversity values, knowledge, and skills on the job?	**Level 3:** Behavior evaluation. Use the post-training survey for managers of participants. For example, the manager fills out a survey based on general impressions of the participant.
Do the managers actually observe and report that participants are using their Diversity values, knowledge, and skills on the job?	**Level 3:** Behavior evaluation. Use the Diversity behavior checklist. For example, the manager keeps a record of observations for one month.
Do managers believe that the organization is benefiting from diversity training?	**Level 4:** Results evaluation. Use the organizational results questionnaire tool.
Does the organization experience specific benefits (financial and non-financial) as a result of the diversity training program?	**Level 5:** Return-on-Investment evaluation. Use the diversity cost and benefit formulas and calculations.

As we explore each diversity training evaluation level, we will answer the following questions:

- What is this technique?

- When is it used?

- What measures are available using this level?

LEVEL 1: PARTICIPANT REACTIONS

What Is This Technique? The purpose of Level 1 evaluation of participants reactions is to find out how the learners feel about the training. It provides a measure of customer satisfaction that is useful for determining whether learners have a positive attitude toward the course and how to improve it if they do not.

The intent of this initial level of evaluation is to measure participant' attitudes and feelings toward:

- ☐ interest and usefulness of the content
- ☐ effectiveness of the instructor
- ☐ quality of the materials

This level of evaluation does not tell you how much participants learned (the learning level does this). However, this level is important because it provides you with continuous feedback for quality improvement. It also provides a forum for participants to air their suggestions, and it helps you produce a course that is satisfying as well as effective.

When Is It Used? Level 1 evaluation is used for almost every training event. A Level 1 questionnaire can be given to the participants at several different times:

- ☐ **End of course.** Having participants fill out the Level 1 measure at the end of the training session while they are still in the classroom is the most common approach.

- ☐ **During the course.** It can also be given at the end of each day during a multiple day program. This gives the instructor and course manager valuable information that can be used to confirm that the course is on the right track or to determine what changes to make the next day. Daily evaluations are useful if you have more than one instructor or speaker. They allow the participants to respond while their reactions are still fresh.

☐ **Shortly after the course.** If it is not feasible to do a Level 1 evaluation while participants are still in the classroom, they can do it within a short time after the course and return it by mail. However, this is less desirable because of uncontrollable factors that can influence responses, and some participants usually do not return questionnaires.

What measures are available using this level?

There are two approaches: one for rating scales and one for open-ended questions.

Rating scales: For each question, add the individual responses and divide by the total number of responses to find the average. This is the most common and useful statistic.

$$= \frac{\text{\# individual responses}}{\text{total responses}}$$

If you want more detail, you can add the total number of each type of response (how many people answered "1," how many answered "2," etc.). This is called a frequency distribution, and it gives you a picture of how similar or different people's attitudes are.

There are other statistics that can be computed, and they are described in other technical books and materials on evaluation. The two described here are sufficient for most purposes.

The scores from the rating scale provide a quantitative measure that is easy to use for making comparisons between individuals or courses.

Each item has a scale ranging from 1 for poor to 5 for excellent. There are also short-answer questions that ask about major strengths, suggestions for improvement, and general comments.

The advantages of the tool in this section is that it can be administered quickly; the process of analyzing participant responses can be automated by using scanning equipment and statistical software packages; and you can compare the results of one course to another. The disadvantage is that it does not give you very much information about the specifics of the course content, goals, instructor, or materials.

Open-ended questions: To analyze the results, you will summarize the answers that participants have given. If it is a small class and the answers are short, you can simply list them in your summary of class activity. When the class is large, or the answers are long, then the procedure is to read them and sort them into groups of similar comments or themes. For each group of similar comments, write a comment or paragraph that captures the key points. You can then list a few of the actual comments or excerpts as examples.

The second Level 1 tool contains items that ask about overall course and materials, instructor effectiveness, potential applications after training, and suggestions for improvement. Most of the items are open-ended, but a few have rating scales.

Variations. You can modify both of the tools discussed here by changing the contents to include the topics of most interest to you and to fit the time allocated for this evaluation. You can also modify the format of the tools by changing open-ended questions to rating scales and vice versa. It all depends on the amount and type of information that you want to receive.

The information that follows illustrates examples of a rating scale and open-ended measurement tool.

PARTICIPANT REACTIONS: RATING SCALE
Reactions to Diversity Training

Instructions: *For each, circle the number that represents your opinion.*

Precourse Preparation

1. My level of understanding of the objectives and job relevance of this course before attending it

1 - Poor   2 - Fair   3 - Good   4 - Very Good   5 - Excellent

Overall Course

2. Level of difficulty of the course

1 - Poor   2 - Fair   3 - Good   4 - Very Good   5 - Excellent

3. The degree to which the course met my expectations

1 - Poor   2 - Fair   3 - Good   4 - Very Good   5 - Excellent

Expectation for Job Transfer

1. Relevancy of the course to my job

1 - Poor   2 - Fair   3 - Good   4 - Very Good   5 - Excellent

Materials/Media

1. Consistency of materials and media with course objectives

1 - Poor   2 - Fair   3 - Good   4 - Very Good   5 - Excellent

Instructor Effectiveness

1. Instructor's ability to deal with conflict in a productive manner

1 - Poor   2 - Fair   3 - Good   4 - Very Good   5 - Excellent

2. Instructor's ability to deal with emotional issues

1 - Poor   2 - Fair   3 - Good   4 - Very Good   5 - Excellent

Short Answer

1. The most beneficial part of the course was:

2. The least beneficial part of the course was:

PARTICIPANT REACTIONS: OPEN-ENDED
Course Evaluation

Instructions: For those question items that use a rating scale, circle the number that best represents your opinion. For all other question items, write your response in the space provided.

Overall Course and Materials

1. Overall, this workshop was:

1 - Poor   2 - Fair   3 - Good   4 - Very Good   5 - Excellent

2. What, if any, aspects of the training were distracting or inhibited your learning?

_____

_____

3. What did the training provide that you did not anticipate?

_____

_____

Instructor Effectiveness

1. Overall, the instructor was:

1 - Poor   2 - Fair   3 - Good   4 - Very Good   5 - Excellent

Application After Training

1. What aspects of this workshop were most relevant to your work?

_____

_____

2. How will you use what you have learned when you return to the job?

_____

_____

LEVEL 2: LEARNING OUTCOMES

What Is This Technique?

Level 2 evaluation is used to find out whether participants have acquired the knowledge, skills, and attitudes described by the course goals and objectives. It provides a measure of accomplishment that can be used for decisions regarding the success of the instructional approach and where improvements might be required.

The most common type of Level 2 tool is an achievement measure such as a test, role play, or exercise. However, in some areas of training, it is not feasible to use achievement measures due to the nature of the course goals, the style of the instructor-participant interactions, or other restrictions. In these cases, a self-report measure of learning can be used.

Level 2 measures complement Level 1 evaluations. Level 1 tells you whether people liked the course but not how much they learned, while Level 2 tells you how much they learned. The organization gains when positive results are achieved on both measures. Low scores on either evaluation can result in negative feedback to other potential participants.

When Is It Conducted?

End of course. Level 2 tools are usually given at the end of a course. However, in management and personal development courses, traditional Level 2 tools are often not used. In these cases, you can use self-report measures, open-ended questions, and activities such as role plays to obtain an estimate of participant accomplishment.

During the course. If it is a modular course, then a Level 2 tool is often used at the end of each module. This allows the instructor and the participants to know whether the objectives are being achieved as they progress through the course. It also removes some of the anxiety from having the total evaluation at the end.

Pretest. Level 2 measures are sometimes taken at the beginning of the course to find out whether learners already know the content. By comparing post-test scores to the pre-test scores, you can find out how much the participants learned in the course.

What Measures Are Available Using This Level?

It is important to know what the result or the outcome is when conducting diversity training. Change can be measured at the individual level in terms of knowledge, skill, or attitude improvement. Comparisons can be made across groups as well.

There are several levels of sophistication in training evaluation. As the degree of sophistication increases, the value tends to go up with it. A few examples of before and after measures, which quantify the results of a diversity training program, are as follows:

Diversity Knowledge Change

$$DKC = \frac{DK_A}{DK_B}$$

Where:
DKC = diversity knowledge change
DK_A = diversity knowledge level after training
DK_B = diversity knowledge level before training

This information can be obtained by pre- and post-testing. Scores can be obtained before and after each class or before and after the total program. This not only serves to demonstrate that people are learning what you want them to learn (*i.e.*, the objectives of the course), but points out specifically by test results what is not being learned. By reviewing the tests in class, you have an opportunity to reinforce the learning. Similar calculations can be used for skill and attitude changes.

Diversity Skill (Behavior) Change

$$DSC = \frac{DS_A}{DS_B}$$

Where:
DSC = observable change in diversity skills as a result of training
DS_A = diversity skill demonstrated after training by work output, critical incidents of interpersonal relations, or other observable phenomena
DS_B = diversity skill level existing previous to the training using the same criteria as above

Data for this diversity skill change ratio can be gathered through questionnaires, interviews, demonstrations, or observation with trainers, subordinates, peers, or supervisors. The key to obtaining something of value from any measure is in being specific in describing the diversity skills or behaviors to be evaluated. You can't put a value on vague explanations, but if you see someone doing something, you can measure and evaluate it.

Diversity Attitude Change

$$DAC = \frac{DA_A}{DA_B}$$

Where:
DAC = diversity attitude change
DA_A = diversity attitude level after training
DA_A = diversity attitude level before training

If the objective is to go beyond knowledge or skill change to attitude change, the same pre- and post-testing method can be used. In this case, either a standard or a specially designed and validated attitude instrument would be used. Since attitudes are particularly vulnerable to influences in the environment, thought should be given to the timing of the post-test. Attitudes immediately after the training may be affected once the participants reenter the work environment. The change may be either positive or negative, and in either case will confound the change attributed to the diversity training program. A test six months after the conclusion of training could tell how much change has been impacted by the environment.

If you find that the environment does not support the new diversity attitudes, it does not make sense to continue to train. Unless you do post-testing, you will never know what happened.

At a perceptual level, four tools can be used for evaluating what participants learned from the training. The first tool is short and uses rating scales. It is used to determine the learning potential of each participant going into the course, whether the specified objectives were covered in the course, and what the participants rate as their personal levels of learning. The participants' learning potential basically asks, did the participant know this material before taking the course, or was there room for improvement?

The accomplishment section asks how the participants perceive their personal accomplishment of that particular objective. This tool provides good statistical data on each participant's perception of accomplishment.

To score this self-assessment, record how many "0's" and "1's" there are under Learning Potential. Then record the total number of "0's" and "1's" under Covered in the Course. For the last column, find the total of the responses and divide by the number who actually answered it.

The second tool is a self-assessment that utilizes rating scales to compare before and after course learning. It asks for the participant's perceptions of their understanding of specific course objectives before and after taking a diversity training course. This tool allows you to see how much improvement there is, and to aggregate scores from a number of classes.

To score this self-assessment, subtract the "before" score from the "after" score. Add all of the remainders for a given item and divide by the total number of responses. Do this for each item.

The next tool is an open-ended questionnaire. Its purpose is to provide participant-generated answers to test their knowledge of the course material. This tool is better than the previous two tools for evaluating what the learner really knows and can recall, because it asks for actual knowledge instead of opinions. This tool takes more time to score than the first two, but it gives the evaluator a specific indication of whether the course objectives are being achieved.

To score this tool, prepare a short list of essential items of information that you are looking for in response to each item and decide how many points to give for each. Five or 10 points per item is a good choice. Depending on the number of questions, you can have a possible total of 50 or 100 points, and there is some latitude for giving partial credit for incomplete answers. Compare the participant's response to this key and give full or partial credit depending on how many key information items are included.

The last tool is a role-play behavioral checklist for diversity training and should be used in conjunction with appropriate role-play activities. The instructor or evaluator can use this tool to evaluate the performance of individuals or groups to determine whether they are exhibiting the appropriate attitudes or behaviors.

To use this tool, prepare for a role play in the normal manner. Once the role play begins, the participants should proceed through the entire scenario without prompting or feedback from the instructor. During the role play, the instructor looks for correct and incorrect examples of behavior related to the objectives in the checklist. For each item, the instructor indicates whether or not it was performed properly. After the scoring is finished, the instructor can then give feedback.

SELF-ASSESSMENT OF LEARNING

Diversity Self-Assessment

Instructions: For each course objective listed below, circle the number that represents your answer to each of the following questions:

Learning Potential: *Was there anything new in this course for you to learn?*

>   0 = I already knew this before the course started

>   1 = At the beginning of the course, I had room for improvement in this area

Covered in the Course: *Was this objective actually taught in the course?*

>   0 = This objective was not covered in the course

>   1 = This objective was covered in the course

Personal Learning Accomplishment: *How well did I learn this objective?*

>   Circle the number that best represents your degree of learning ranging from:

1 = For little or no change

5 = If you believe that you achieved a satisfactory level of mastery

COURSE OBJECTIVES	LEARNING POTENTIAL		COVERED IN COURSE?		HOW WELL I LEARNED THIS IN THE COURSE				
As a result of taking this course, I am able to:					Little or None		Improved My Skill		Achieved Mastery
1. Identify demographic trends that have a strong impact on quality of work life, and workers	0	1	0	1	1	2	3	4	5
2. Define stereotyping, racism, sexism	0	1	0	1	1	2	3	4	5
3. Recognize the primary dimensions of perceived differences in cultural groups	0	1	0	1	1	2	3	4	5
4. Identify situations and employee responses that typically result in intercultural conflicts	0	1	0	1	1	2	3	4	5

The following tool provides a "before" and "after" self-assessment of learning. You can subtract the first score from the second one to determine how much participants have changed.

Diversity Pre- and Post-Course Self-Assessment

Instructions: Circle the number that represents your choice.

COURSE OBJECTIVES	BEFORE TAKING THE CLASS	AFTER TAKING THE CLASS
As a result of taking this course, I am able to:	Before taking the diversity training course, my level of knowledge or competency for this objective was	After taking the diversity training course my level of knowledge or competency for this objective is
1. Recognize cultural stereotyping and biases toward race, gender, ethnicity, physical characteristic, and other differences	1 2 3 4 5 LOW MODERATE HIGH	1 2 3 4 5 LOW MODERATE HIGH
Understand my own cultural conditioning and how that may consciously or unconsciously influence my interactions with others	1 2 3 4 5 LOW MODERATE HIGH	1 2 3 4 5 LOW MODERATE HIGH

KNOWLEDGE OF DIVERSITY ISSUES

Assessment of Diversity-Related Knowledge

Instructions: For each question, write your answer in the space provided.

1. What are the advantages for using diversity training in the workplace?

_____

_____

2. What are the definitions of culture, ethnicity, prejudice, sexism, and racism?

_____

_____

3. What are your responsibilities in dealing with issues of diversity?

_____

_____

LEARNING OUTCOMES ROLE PLAY

Diversity Role Play Checklist

Group#_____ Group Members:_____

Instructor:_____ Course:_____

Instructions: For each skill, indicate whether or not it was demonstrated by the participant(s) by circling the appropriate number.

SKILL	DEMONSTRATED	COMMENTS
1. Recognize and responded to instances of stereotyping and biased decision making within the work group.	0=NO 1=Yes	

SKILL	DEMONSTRATED	COMMENTS
2. Used strategies to counteract instances of bias in the work group	0=NO 1=Yes	
3. Informed others of unbiased and biased attitudes in a constructive manner	0=NO 1=Yes	
4. Displayed behaviors which are characteristic of effective and united teams	0=NO 1=Yes	

LEVEL 3: TRANSFER OF TRAINING

What Is This Technique?
One of the primary goals of diversity training is to improve employee opportunity and performance on the job. The purpose of Level 3 evaluation is to find out whether course participants have transferred their newly-learned diversity knowledge, skills, and values to the job. This helps you determine how effective the course is, where to make improvements, how to further build workforce satisfaction, and improve productivity.

It is also useful, whenever possible, to find out why transfer has or has not occurred. Failure to transfer can be caused by things other than lack of learning. For example, successful transfer requires additional coaching and support on the job. If this does not happen, or if employees simply do not get the opportunity to use what they have learned, then you will not see transfer even though they may have learned the skills in your diversity course. In these cases, the course might be working just fine, and improvements are needed in the workplace to encourage and support transfer.

When Is It? Used

Level 3 evaluation takes place after the course is completed and participants have had enough time to demonstrate their attitudes and skills on the job. This can occur immediately after training, but usually takes longer for nontechnical skills such as diversity.

☐ **Immediate transfer.** When the learning outcomes are highly related to job performance, then transfer may occur almost immediately. Even if it does, it is important to determine whether the transfer continues to operate over a longer period of time or stops due to insufficient training or lack of support on the job.

☐ **One to three months after training.** Other kinds of training can require one to three months before evidence of transfer occurs. These include complex skills involving management and human interactions, or development skills that require time and practice to mature. Some of the diversity attitudes and skills could transfer rather quickly, but others would require a longer time. This is because it takes time to learn how to use the new attitudes and skills in the actual work environment, and situations that call for some of these skills might not occur frequently. The best time for Level 3 evaluation of diversity training is probably one to three months after the course.

What Measures Are

Participant Post-Training Surveys. This section contains tools that evaluate the effectiveness with

Available Using This Level?

which employees are taking new skills back to the job. The purpose of the format is to provide employees and their managers with similar evaluation tools, then compare the results to get the two perceptions. With parallel evaluation forms, it is easier to directly compare results from specific questions without loss of interpretation.

The first tool is the longest and most detailed in this section, and it parallels one of the other tools in the manager's post-training section. Here the participants are asked to circle the appropriate response regarding how well the course prepared them, how frequently they use the new attitude or skill, and how important it is to their job responsibilities. This tool will provide good statistical data, especially when paired with its management counterpart, and reveal perceptual similarities and differences between the employee and the manager.

Manager's Post-Training Evaluations. The tools in this section can be used as stand-alone measuring devices or in conjunction with their counterparts.

The second tool is a long stand-alone tool that combines the characteristics of the ranked and open-ended question type. This format provides numerical results for statistical analysis as well as verbal responses to add specificity.

The third tool parallels the first tool in the participant post-training section. It is intended to provide a detailed method for comparing perceptions of the employee and the manager. Again, the viewpoint was changed to focus on the manager's observation of the employee. Besides the removal of the Prepared column, all other instructions are the same.

The last tool is a diversity checklist. This tool is designed to be used by managers to record whether they actually observed an employee using diversity attitudes and behaviors. Specific behavioral objectives that the employee should be applying to the job are listed on the left. Through observation, managers can record the date they observed that particular behavior, the level of satisfaction in performing the behavior, and their comments and suggestions. This tool is particularly helpful to track various employees' uses of the different skills learned in the diversity training course.

In some organizations, employee-manager contact is limited. If the employee's manager is not in a position to observe the employee on a regular basis, alternative methods and tools should be used. In some situations, this tool can be adapted to be used with other individuals who have regular contact with the employee, such as peers, subordinates, and customers.

Participant Tool

PARTICIPANT POST-TRAINING SURVEY

Applying Diversity Training On-the-Job: Participant Version

For each task listed below, please indicate how well the training course prepared you, how often you actually use it, and the importance of this skill to your job responsibilities.

Instructions: Circle the appropriate number in the column that represents your opinion.

SPECIFIC TASK	PREPARED How well did the course prepare you to perform this task?	USE How often do you use this knowledge or skill on the job?	IMPORTANCE How important is this skill or knowledge to your job?
1. Create an inclusive work environment where individuals are treated fairly	0= Poorly 1= Somewhat 2= Very Well	0= Seldom 1= Sometimes 2= Very Often	0= Not At All 1= Somewhat 2= Very Much

SPECIFIC TASK	PREPARED How well did the course prepare you to perform this task?	USE How often do you use this knowledge or skill on the job?	IMPORTANCE How important is this skill or knowledge to your job?
2. Analyze diverse viewpoints to make planning decisions and solve work problems	0= Poorly 1= Somewhat 2= Very Well	0= Seldom 1= Sometimes 2= Very Often	0= Not At All 1= Somewhat 2= Very Much
3. Values and encourage open communication, input opinions, and ideas from others	0= Poorly 1= Somewhat 2= Very Well	0= Seldom 1= Sometimes 2= Very Often	0= Not At All 1= Somewhat 2= Very Much
4. Model trust, openness, fairness, and respect for the individual in daily behavior	0= Poorly 1= Somewhat 2= Very Well	0= Seldom 1= Sometimes 2= Very Often	0= Not At All 1= Somewhat 2= Very Much

Manager's Tool

MANAGER'S POST-TRAINING SURVEY

Satisfaction with Diversity Training Course Effectiveness

Instructions: Circle the number that best reflects your opinion. Add comments whenever possible. This information will help us estimate the effectiveness of the diversity training and improve it.

For each of the following behaviors, please rate your satisfaction with your employee's performance:

1. Works effectively with people of different race, gender, and sexual orientation

1	2	3	4	5
Not Satisfied		Satisfied		Very Satisfied

2. Combats prejudice and discrimination

1	2	3	4	5
Not Satisfied		Satisfied		Very Satisfied

3. Responds sensitively to ideas or behaviors that differ from those of the dominant culture

1	2	3	4	5
Not Satisfied		Satisfied		Very Satisfied

4. Creates a climate in which everyone is respected and treated fairly regardless of race, age, gender, religion, disability, color, or sexual orientation

1	2	3	4	5
Not Satisfied		Satisfied		Very Satisfied

5. Overall, how satisfied are you that the Diversity Training Course provided skills and values that are relevant to the workplace?

1	2	3	4	5
Not Satisfied		Satisfied		Very Satisfied

Comments:

6. Overall, how satisfied are you with your employees' ability to apply skills and values that they learned in Diversity Training?

1	2	3	4	5
Not Satisfied		Satisfied		Very Satisfied

Comments:_____

MANAGER'S POST-TRAINING SURVEY
Applying Diversity Training On-the-Job: Manager's Version

For each task listed below, please indicate how often your employees actually use these skills and how important they are to his/her job responsibilities.

Instructions: Circle the number in each column that represents your opinion.

SPECIFIC TASK	USE How often does your employee use this skill?	IMPORTANCE Is this skill important to his/her job responsibilities?
1. Create an inclusive work environment where individuals are treated fairly	1=Almost Never 2=Seldom 3=Usually 4=Almost Always	0=No 1=Somewhat 2=Very Much
2. Analyze diverse viewpoints to make planning decisions and solve work problems	1=Almost Never 2=Seldom 3=Usually 4=Almost Always	0=No 1=Somewhat 2=Very Much
3. Values and encourage open communication, input, opinions, and ideas from others.	1=Almost Never 2=Seldom 3=Usually 4=Almost Always	0=No 1=Somewhat 2=Very Much
4. Model trust, openness, fairness, and respect for the individual in daily behavior	1=Almost Never 2=Seldom 3=Usually 4=Almost Always	0=No 1=Somewhat 2=Very Much

DIVERSITY BEHAVIOR CHECKLIST

Performance Checklist for Diversity Training Transfer

Reviewed Employee:_____ Diversity Course:_____

Reviewing Supervisor:_____ Current Date:_____

Period of Observation: Start:_____ Stop:_____

Instructions: Respond to the following items for each skill:

Dates Observed: *What day did you observe the employee perform the skill?* List the dates on which you observed the skill being performed. If you observed the skill more than once on a given day, repeat the date for each observation.

Performance Rating: *How well did s/he perform the skill?* If you observed the skill, circle the appropriate number in the second column that best represents your overall assessment of the employee's performance.

Comments: Please provide any additional information which you feel is important in the third column (*e.g.*, unusual circumstances, environmental factors, or details about the performance).

SKILL TO BE REVIEWED	DATES	PERFORMANCE RATING	COMMENTS
1. Encourages pride, trust, and group identity		1=Needs Improvement 2 3=Satisfactory 4 5=Very Competent	

SKILL TO BE REVIEWED	DATES	PERFORMANCE RATING	COMMENTS
2. Treats people fairly and equitably		1=Needs Improvement 2 3=Satisfactory 4 5=Very Competent	
3. Values and capitalizes on team's diverse skills and backgrounds.		1=Needs Improvement 2 3=Satisfactory 4 5=Very Competent	

Performance Change

Another means of measuring level 3 transfer of training is to monitor changes in diverse work group performance appraisal ratings in relationship to receiving diversity training.

$$PC = \frac{PA}{PB}$$

Where:

PC = change in work performance as measured by the organization's performance appraisal system

P_A = latest review score from a performance appraisal conducted at least 90 days after the diversity training

P_B = performance review score from the performance appraisal conducted prior to the diversity training

Since performance appraisal scales are usually small (*e.g.*, 1 through 5 or 1 through 6), the difference in a single point may appear dramatic in terms of percentage change. Caution should be exercised in discussing an individual's performance change or you may be accused of overstatement. This measure takes on more meaning when a large number of appraisals are compared and consistently positive results appear.

A word of warning. There may be a halo effect. That is, the evaluator knows the employee went through training and expects improved performance. If the evaluator is not careful, something that is not there may be inferred.

LEVEL 4: ORGANIZATIONAL RESULTS

What Is This Technique? The ultimate purpose of training is to help the organization achieve its goals. This means that, in addition to transferring new skills/attitudes to the job, the results of training must have a positive effect on the organization. For example, let's assume that people show the desirable diversity behaviors at work. They are sensitive to their biases and overcome them by treating people as individuals. The next question is whether this results in desirable organizational performance that meets diversity objectives such as:

☐ Everyone feeling like they are part of the work team

☐ Fewer problems and grievances

☐ Higher productivity, morale, etc.

If training was the appropriate solution to this problem, or an important part of the solution, then we would expect to see these organizational benefits. This is the purpose of Level 4 evaluation.

Level 4 evaluation can occur at several levels. The first is the perceptual level. As with other levels of evaluation, it is possible to discover whether people perceive improvements in the expected areas of change. The second is performance, which is used to determine whether there are measurable improvements in organizational performance. The final level is financial. It uses processes for estimating whether there is a financial gain when the costs of training are compared to measurable benefits. These financial measures are the focus of Level 5: Return on Investment.

The focus of our examination of Level 4 measures will be concentrated at the perceptual level.

When Is It Used?

Like Level 3 evaluation, Level 4 is undertaken after the course has ended. Usually the time lapse is longer than for Level 3 evaluation. This is because organizational results occur sometime after the skills are actually transferred to the job. Typically the interval is three to six months after training, but in some cases it may be as long as nine to 12 months after training. (It can be sooner if there is reason to believe that changes could occur in less time.)

What Measures Are Available Using This Level?

Organizational Results Survey. This tool is used to measure how much effect the training has had on the organizational environment and practice. This survey lists some possible organizational impacts the training can have, and provides a rating scale that asks if the evaluator (often the manager) agrees or does not agree that these impacts have occurred. This higher level evaluation will assist management in determining if the training has had the desired organizational impact. It is an effective way to gauge the perceptual return on training investment for the organization.

ORGANIZATIONAL RESULTS SURVEY

Organizational Impact Evaluation

Instructions: Rate each item by circling the number that represents your opinion.

ORGANIZATIONAL RESULTS	RATING				
	Strongly Disagree		Somewhat Agree		Strongly Agree
1. Diversity is part of the everyday communication at all employee levels.	1	2	3	4	5
2. Managers and employees are able to communicate about differences more freely.	1	2	3	4	5
3. The work climate for women, minorities, and other members of diverse groups has improved.	1	2	3	4	5
4. Women, minorities, and other members of diverse groups feel part of the work team.	1	2	3	4	5
5. The selection rates of qualified women, minorities, and other members of diverse groups for hiring and promotions has increased.	1	2	3	4	5

ORGANIZATIONAL RESULTS	RATING				
	Strongly Disagree		Somewhat Agree		Strongly Agree
6. The diversity of the work force has increased.	1	2	3	4	5
7. Employees are taking personal responsibility for monitoring the work environment and responding to cases of discrimination and harassment.	1	2	3	4	5
8. Managers are taking personal responsibility for monitoring the work environment and responding to cases of discrimination and harassment.	1	2	3	4	5
9. The work environment does not tolerate racism, sexism, and insensitive behavior toward members of diverse groups.	1	2	3	4	5
10. After the training, there might have been an initial increase in discrimination complaints, but there was adecline over time.	1	2	3	4	5

Level 5: Return on Training Investment

What Is This Technique?

Possibly the ultimate level of evaluation is to compare the financial benefits of a program to the cost of that program. This comparison is the elusive goal of many diversity professionals.

First, you must have useful techniques to assign values to program data, particularly in those areas where it is fairly difficult. Data must be transformed into dollar values before the financial benefit can be calculated. This includes exploring calculations such as the value of increased output (*e.g.*, the average dollar sale, average profit per sale, etc), the value of cost savings (*e.g.*, actual savings in raw materials, supplies, time value of money), the value of time savings (*e.g.*, wages/salaries and benefits saved, reduced training time, penalty avoidance), the value of improved quality (*e.g.*, error reduction, increased accuracy, reduced waste, reduced rework, improved morale, reduced mistakes), and the value of "soft" data (*e.g.*, existing data/historical costs, expert opinion, participant estimation of values/costs, management estimation of values/costs).

Second, the methods of comparisons can be explored, the most common being return on investment (ROI). Using this procedure, Return on Training Investment can be calculated as well as other important measures.

When Is It Used?

Like Level 4 evaluation, Level 5 is undertaken after the course has ended. Usually the time lapse is the same as Level 4 or slightly longer to align with organizational data reporting periods.

The calculation of the return for a Diversity training program is not feasible or realistic in all cases. Even if the perceived benefits have been converted to dollar savings, the mere calculation of the return communicates to a perceptive manager more preciseness in the evaluation than may be there. Usually, the ROI calculation should be used when the program benefits can be clearly documented and substantiated, even if they are subjective. If management believes in the method of calculating the benefits, then they will have confidence in the value for the return. The nature of the program can also have a bearing on whether or not it makes sense to calculate a return. Management may believe, without question, an ROI calculation for sales training programs focused on diverse market penetration. They can easily see how an improvement can be documented and a value tied to it.

On the other hand, an ROI for a program that teaches managers the principles of transactional analysis for diversity may be difficult to swallow--even for the most understanding management staff. Therefore, the key considerations are reliability of the data and credibility of the conclusions based upon subjective data.

What Measures Are Available Using This Level?

The return on investment is an important calculation for diversity professionals. Yet, it is a figure that must be used with caution and care. There are many ways that it can be interpreted or misinterpreted. This section gives some general guidelines to help calculate a return, interpret its meaning, and calculate other costs and benefits.

Defining Return on Investment

Return on investment (ROI) may appear to be improper terminology for the diversity field. The expression originates in finance and accounting and usually refers to the pre-tax contribution measured against controllable assets. In formula form it is expressed as:

$$\text{Average ROI} = \frac{\text{pretax earnings}}{\text{average investment}}$$

It measures the anticipated profitability of an investment and is used as a standard measure of the performance of divisions or profit centers within a business.

The investment portion of the formula represents capital expenditures such as a training facility or equipment plus initial development or production costs. The original investment figure or production costs can be used. Also, the original investment figure can be used, or the present book value can be expressed as the average investment over a period of time. If the diversity program is a one-time offering, then the figure is the original investment.

However, if the initial costs are spread over a period of time, then the average book value is usually more appropriate. This value is essentially half the initial costs since, through depreciation, a certain fixed part of investment is written off each year over the life of the investment.

In many situations a group of employees are to be trained at one time, so the investment figure is the total cost of analysis, development, delivery, and evaluation lumped together for the bottom part of the equation. The benefits are then calculated assuming that all participants attend the program or have attended the program, depending on whether the return is a prediction or a reflection of what has happened.

To keep calculations simple, it is recommended that the return be based on pretax conditions. This avoids the issue of investment tax credits, depreciation, tax shields, and other related items.

To illustrate this calculation, assume that a work-life and family training program had initial costs of $50,000. The program will have a useful life of three years with negligible residual value at that time.

During the three-year period, the program produces a net savings of $30,000, or $10,000 per year ($30,000/3). The average investment is $25,000 ($50,000/2) since the average book value is essentially half the costs. The average return is:

$$\text{Average ROI} \quad = \quad \frac{\text{annual savings}}{\text{average investment}}$$

$$= \quad \frac{\$10,000}{\$25,000}$$

$$= \quad 40\%$$

Return on investment is sometimes used loosely to represent the return on assets (ROA) or the return on equity (ROE). Equity usually refers to the net worth of an organization. The assets represent the total assets employed to generate earnings, including debt. The ROA and ROE are terms that are more meaningful when evaluating the entire organization or a division. ROI is usually sufficient for evaluating expenditures relating to a diversity program.

Finance and accounting personnel may take issue with calculations involving the return on investment for efforts such as a diversity program. Nevertheless, the expression is fairly common and conveys an adequate meaning of financial evaluation.

Some professionals suggest a more appropriate name is return on training. Others avoid the word "return" and would simply calculate the dollar savings as a result of the program, which is basically the benefits minus costs. These figures may be more meaningful to managers to keep from getting the ROI calculation confused with similar calculations for capital expenditures.

ROI may be calculated prior to a diversity program to estimate the potential cost effectiveness or after a program has been conducted to measure the results achieved. The methods of calculation are the same. However, the estimated return before a program is usually calculated for a proposal to implement the program. The data for its calculation are more subjective and usually less reliable than the data after the program is completed. Because of this factor, management may require a higher ROI for a diversity program in the proposal stage.

MEASUREMENT BY THE NUMBERS IS REQUIRED

If you want to measure the effects and value of training at any level, you can. You can even put a dollar value on the impact. The approaches discussed here are proof that no matter what type of diversity training has been applied, it can be measured and evaluated. The most important requirement is that you follow the principles and steps described in this section.

If it were easy to measure diversity training effects, many more people would be doing this as a matter of routine. However, there is distance still to be traveled and much to be learned. When we start to show management exactly how much value diversity training programs can contribute to the process of building an inclusive work environment, the programs will become a strategic requirement.

CHAPTER 9 Diversity Staff and Style: Developing Personnel and Cultural Measures

INTRODUCTION

When it comes to diversity measurement, recruiting activities and cultural audits using organizational surveys ranks high among the list of the most frequently used methods. For organizations interested in measuring the results of their Diversity Staffing and Style dimensions, there are a wealth of measures available to accurately monitor and manage these activities.

In this chapter, we will examine measures covering the Diversity Staff and Style dimensions of the Diversity 9-S Framework.

MEASURES WHICH SUPPORT THESE DIMENSIONS:
DIVERSITY STAFF AND STYLE

The following diversity measures will be discussed in this chapter. These measures are not intended to be exhaustive, however, they do reflect some possible measures to use in each area.

STAFF MEASURES

1. Time-to Fill (explained in chapter three)

2. Cost per Diversity Hire

3. Source Cost per Diversity Hire (explained in chapter six)

4. Diversity Hit Rate

5. Diversity Hire Referral Rate

6. Diversity Hire Performance Impact

7. Average Tenure By Diversity Grouping versus Former Employees

8. Diversity Stability Factor, Diversity Instability Factor

9. Diversity Survivor Rate, Diversity Loss Rate

Style Measures

1. Diversity Feedback Items in Employee Opinion Survey
   (see Organizational Results Survey in Chapter Eight)

2. Stratified Focus Group Feedback Benchmarks

3. % of favorable responses on Organizational Culture Audit as compared to previous years, other parts of organization and industry

4. # of Minorities and Women in Key Management and Leadership

Positions

5. 5x5 Study - 5 years at level 5 performance

6. $ and % of Budget Allocated to Diversity Initiatives

7. Organizational Mentoring Analysis

Now, let's explore the measures which support the Diversity Staff and Style dimensions of the Diversity "9-S" Framework.

ANALYZING THE DIVERSITY STAFF DIMENSION

The following information provides an overview of the diversity measures and associated formulas that can be used to monitor the Diversity Staff dimension.

Staff Measure-1

ELEMENT	APPLICATION
Diversity Measure	**Cost Per Diversity Hire**
Measure Description	This measure is designed help you analyze the cost to bring on each diversity hire. At first blush, the Cost per Diversity Hire measure can be thought to consist of only direct costs for advertising and agency fees. However, when you dig deeper, there are a number of other costs associated with this measure. These costs are described below.
Suggested Use/Purpose	To examine staffing costs by diversity dimension.

ELEMENT	APPLICATION
Formula Elements	$$CPDH = \frac{(Ad + AF + ER + T + Relo + RC) + 10\%}{DH}$$ Where: • CPDH = cost per diversity hire • Ad = advertising fees paid to generate applicants (*e.g.*, $12,000) • AF = agency fees paid to generate applicants from an agency or non traditional recruiting source, and even temporary workers (*e.g.*, $6,000). • ER = employee referral bonus for current employees who bring in qualified applicants (*e.g.*, $1000). • T = travel expenses associated with hire (*e.g.*, $5,000) • Relo = relocation expenses associated with hire (*e.g.*, $22,000). • RC = recruiters' salary and benefits costs multiplied by the number of hours spent spent per job (*e.g.*, $9,000) • +10% = all other staff time—*e.g.*, clerks, hiring department staff and management is part of the 10 percent miscellaneous cost variable. • DH = total diversity hires (*e.g.*, 35)
Example	$$CPDH = \frac{(Ad + AF + ER + T + Relo + RC) + 10\%}{DH}$$ $$= \frac{12000 + 1000 + 6000 + 5000 + 15000 + 9000) + 10\%}{35}$$ $$= \frac{\$52800}{35}$$ $$= \$1508.57$$ **Note:** Quite often positions may be filled without incurring any significant travel and relocation expenses. Then all of a sudden you may spend $25,000 or more on one diversity hire (especially a management

ELEMENT	APPLICATION

hire). If you simply throw that one person in with the 10 preceding diversity hires, where you spent less than $5,000 total, the resulting average cost per diversity hire will be skewed. The number will be misleading and totally non-indicative of what has happened over the last 11 diversity hires.

The $25,000 will be added to the total cost of hiring for the month. However, it will probably be appropriate to report two sets of figures. One would be those hires that did not require relocation. The other would be those in which there were relocations. Not only is this more truthful, it provides management with an appreciation for the impact of relocation expenses on the bottom-line. Your job is not only to show management how effectively you are managing the diversity change process, it is also imperative to show them how the job could be done better. If you can come up with a plan to improve or leverage local resources for diverse work force talent, you can probably get support for it.

Recruiters' salary and benefits costs is multiplied by the number of hours spent per job.

All other staff time—*e.g.*, clerks, hiring department staff and management—is part of the 10 percent miscellaneous cost variable. As such, I wouldn't recommend that you spend a lot of time working it out. However, if you feel you must, here's a few tips.

The calculation and allocation of staff time can also quickly become an indecipherable mess unless you establish an accounting method and stay with it. The simplest way to reduce this problem to a manageable and understandable variable is to introduce standard labor costing. By borrowing a leaf from manufacturing's book, you can determine the normal cost of an employee hour of work and set that as your standard rate. For example, a clerk's standard rate could be

ELEMENT	APPLICATION
	determined in the following manner:

Salary (converted to hourly rate)	$8.25
Benefits (30% of salary)	2.93
Overhead charge (space, equipment, etc.)	4.65
Total	**$15.83**

The standard rate you will apply to all staff time calculations where a clerk is involved would be $15.83. In time you will be able to develop an average number of hours that a clerk puts in on a given group of hires. Let's say, as an example, you find that the clerk spends 1½ hours on the average per diversity hire. If you multiply $15.83 times 1½ the product is $28.75, which becomes the standard cost of an employment clerk's time for each diversity hire that the clerk assists in hiring. Multiply $28.75 times the number of hires that month and you have one component of the total month's cost of hiring. The same process is then applied to recruiters, receptionists, records clerks, and anyone else in the department who is involved in hiring. You may even choose to allocate a portion of your time as diversity manager. The process may need to be recomputed for different types or levels of jobs since it usually takes more time to hire managerial employees versus first-level employees.

ELEMENT	APPLICATION
Key Analysis or Processing Questions Examine for this Measure	1. How does this dollar amount compare by department, division, or region? 2. How does this figure compare with others in our industry? Our competition? 3. What are the business implications and consequences of this number based upon the organization's strategic objectives? 4. What should our next steps be in light of this information? Why? When? Who? How? What Barriers exist?

Staff Measure-2

ELEMENT	APPLICATION
Diversity Measure	**Diversity Hit Rate**
Measure Description	This measure helps you to indicate how productive your recruiting efforts are. Simply stated, hit rate is the ratio of job offers made to job offers accepted.
Suggested Use/Purpose	To measure recruiting productivity.
Formula Elements	$DHO = \dfrac{OA}{OE}$ Where: · DHO = percentage of offers that result in a Diversity hire. · OA = offers accepted (*e.g.*, 42) · OE = offers extended (*e.g.*, 50)
Example	$DHO = \dfrac{42}{50}$ $= 84\%$
Key Analysis or Processing Questions Examine for this Measure	1. What is the percentage? 2. How does this percentage compare by department, division, or region? 3. How does this figure compare with others in our industry? Our competition? 4. What are the business implications and consequences of this number based upon the organization's strategic objectives? 5. What should our next steps be in light of this information? Why? When? Who? How? What Barriers exist?

Staffing Measure-3

ELEMENT	APPLICATION
Diversity Measure	**Diversity Hire Referral Rate**
Measure Description	This measure helps you examine the rate at which diversity candidates are referred to the organization.
Suggested Use/Purpose	To measure referrals. As market conditions change, referral rates generally change accordingly. It is critical to monitor this process in conjunction with changes in market conditions.
Formula Elements	$$DHRR = \frac{R}{O}$$ Where: • DHRR = diversity referral factor, relationship of candidates to openings. • R = number of candidates referred for interview (*e.g.*, 76) • O = number of openings (*e.g.*, 22)
Example	$$DHRR = \frac{76}{22}$$ $$= 3.5$$
Key Analysis or Processing Questions Examine for this Measure	1. What is the number? 2. How does this number compare by department, division, or region? 3. How does this figure compare with others in our industry? Our competition? 4. What are the business implications and consequences of this number based upon the organization's strategic objectives? 5. What should our next steps be in light of this information? Why? When? Who? How? What Barriers exist?

Staffing Measure-4

ELEMENT	APPLICATION
Measure	**Diversity Hire Performance Impact**
Measure Description	This measure reflects the performance quality of the diversity hiree. This performance quality impact is designed to help you indicate whether the diversity hire is adding performance value to the organization.
Suggested Use/Purpose	Quality is a function of use over time. When an employee joins the organization and begins to work you can assess performance, but that requires waiting. Patience is a prerequisite to measuring performance quality. Flash-in-the-pan assessments must be avoided. For example, some new employees may look great for the first few months, until they feel secure. After about six months the true nature of the individual may become more visible. Therefore, taking measurements after that time may be more reliable. Performance on the job, promotion to higher levels and stability are all measures that cannot be measured for a minimum of six months. Whenever we think of product quality we expect a product to do what it is supposed to do, perform its function for a long time, and last.
Formula Elements	$$DHPI = \frac{DHPR+DHP+DHS}{N}$$ Where: • DHPI = diversity hire performance impact • DHPR = average job performance rating of new diversity hires (*e.g.*, 4 points out of 5 point performance rating scale = 80%) • DHP = Percentage of new diversity hirees promoted within one year (*e.g.*, 45%)

ELEMENT	APPLICATION
	• DHS = Percentage of new diversity hirees retained after one year (*e.g.*, 90%) • N = number of indicators used (*e.g.*, 3)
Example	$$\text{DHPI} = \frac{80+45+90}{3}$$ $$= \frac{215}{3}$$ $$= 71.7\%$$ The resulting percentage, 71.7 percent is a relative value. You must determine whether this value represents high, medium, or low quality. This comparison can be based on historical comparisons, preset performance standards or objectives, or management mandates.
Key Analysis or Processing Questions Examine for this Measure	1. How does this figure compare with this same period last year, last month, Over the last three years? Why? 2. Is the trend going down, up, staying the same? Why? 3. How does this trend or figure compare with others in our industry? Our competition? 4. What are the business implications and consequences of this number based upon the organization's strategic objectives? 5. How does this number compare with Best Practices Standards for this type of data? 6. What should our next steps be in light of this information? Why? When? Who? How? What Barriers exist?

ELEMENT	APPLICATION
Possible Graphic	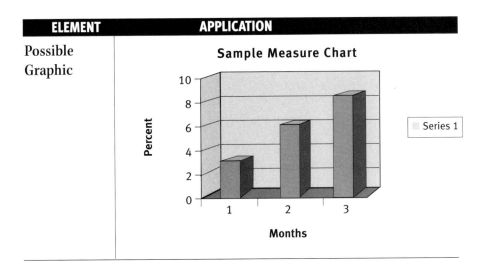

Staffing Measure-5

ELEMENT	APPLICATION
Measure	**Average Tenure By Diversity Grouping versus Former Employees**
Measure Description	This measure reflects the average length of service of all current diversity group employees who stay versus the average length of service of all diversity group employees who departed from the organization.
Suggested Use/Purpose	This measure examines the range of employee tenure by diversity grouping and help to highlight the rate the organization may be losing diverse work force talent.
Formula Elements	$$SS = \dfrac{TSS}{E}$$ $$SL = \dfrac{TSL}{E}$$

ELEMENT	APPLICATION
	Where: • SS = average length of service of current employees—stayers • TSS = total sum of years of service of all staying employees (*e.g.*, 112,025) • SL = average length of service of departed employees—leavers •TSL = total sum of years of service of all departed employees (*e.g.*, 16,589) • E = total number of employees in that group (*e.g.*, stayers = 2041; leavers = 1056)
Example	$$SS = \frac{112,025}{2041} \qquad SL = \frac{16,589}{1056}$$ $$= \quad 5.5 \text{ years} \qquad\qquad 1.6 \text{ years}$$ This calculation suggests that most employees who leave have relatively short tenure with the organization. We know from experience that the longer an employee stays with an organization, the more likely they are to continue to stay. Another way to put it is that most of the voluntary turnover occurs within the first two years of service. This calculation can be computed by diversity group to examine differences and trends that may be in place. The key will be to find out why this is occurring.
Key Analysis or Processing Questions Examine for this Measure	1. How do these figures compare with this same period last year, last month, Over the last three years? Why? 2. Is the trend going down, up, staying the same? Why? 3. How does this trend or figure compare with others in our industry? Our competition? 4. What are the business implications and consequences of this number based upon the organization's strategic objectives?

ELEMENT	APPLICATION
	5. How does this number compare with Best Practices Standards for this type of data?
	6. What should our next steps be in light of this information? Why? When? Who? How? What Barriers exist?
Possible Graphic	**Average Turnover By Diversity Grouping** *(line chart: Y-axis "Years" from 0 to 8; X-axis "Group" from 1 to 5; two series — Stayers and Leavers)*

Staffing Measure-6

ELEMENT	APPLICATION
Measure	**Diversity Stability Factor, Diversity Instability Factor**
Measure Description	Stability calculations tell you whether or not the turnover rate for a given population, *i.e.*, diverse work group employees with over five years of service, is changing. It answers questions such as "Are our minority or female employees leaving at the same rate as other groups? This can be calculated from either side, as stability or instability rates.
Suggested Use/Purpose	This measure is very useful for a wide range of turnover comparisons by group.

ELEMENT	APPLICATION
Formula Elements	$SF = \dfrac{OS}{E}$ $IF = \dfrac{OL}{E}$ Where: · SF = stability factor of an existing population. · OS = original employees who remain for the period, for example, 1 year (*e.g.*, 832) · IF = instability factor of an existing population. · OL = original employees who left during the period (*e.g.*, 80) · E = employee population at the beginning of the period (*e.g.*, 912)
Example	$SF = \dfrac{832}{912}$ $\qquad$ $IF = \dfrac{80}{912}$ $= 91.2\%$ $\qquad\qquad = 8.8\%$ Obviously, SF and IF are reciprocals. In this case, 91.2 percent of the employees with over five years of service stayed and 8.8 percent left during the past year. This can be compared with your previous experience during the past year as indicated in the key analysis questions shown below.
Key Analysis or Processing Questions Examine for this Measure	1. How does this figure compare with this same period last year, last month, Over the last three years? Why? 2. Is the trend going down, up, staying the same? Why? 3. How does this trend or figure compare with others in our industry? Our competition? 4. What are the business implications and consequences of this number based upon the organization's strategic objectives? 5. How does this number compare with Best Practices Standards for this type of data?

ELEMENT	APPLICATION
	6. What should our next steps be in light of this information? Why? When? Who? How? What Barriers exist?
Possible Graphic	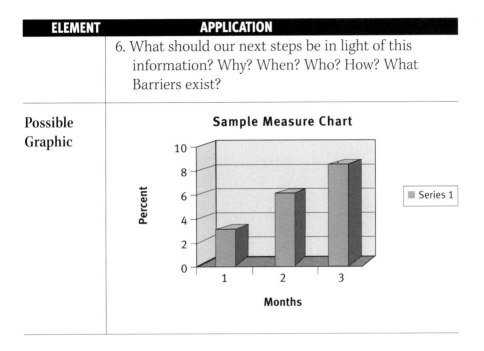

Staffing Measure-7

ELEMENT	APPLICATION
Measure	**Diversity Survival Rate, Diversity Loss Rate**
Measure Description	Survival or loss rates of new hires is conceptually identical to stability and instability factor, only here the base population is new hires and not existing employee groups. A time period, say a month or a quarter, is defined, and all hires during that period are counted. At some point in the future, perhaps six months or one year later, all hires from the base period are traced and counted, either as stayers or leavers. The formulae that follow highlight how this is computed.

ELEMENT	APPLICATION
Formula Elements	$SR = \dfrac{HS}{H}$ $LR = \dfrac{HL}{H}$ Where: • SR = survival rate of new hires • HS = number of new hires from the period who are still employed, stayers (*e.g.*, 209) • LR = Loss rate or wastage • HL = number of new hires who left, leavers (*e.g.*, 79) • H = total number of new hires during the period (*e.g.*, 288)
Example	$SR = \dfrac{209}{288}$ $LR = \dfrac{79}{288}$ = 72.6% = 27.4% This measure can also be used to examine a portion of a diversity recruiter's effectiveness. However, since a new hire's survival is out of the hands of the recruiter, this measures should be used with caution!!
Key Analysis or Processing Questions Examine for this Measure	1. How does this figure compare with this same period last month, Over the last three years? Why? 2. Is the trend going down, up, staying the same? Why? 3. How does this trend or figure compare with others in our industry? Our competition? 4. What are the business implications and consequences of this number based upon the organization's strategic objectives? 5. How does this number compare with Best Practices Standards for this type of data? 6. What should our next steps be in light of this information? Why? When? Who? How? What Barriers exist?

ELEMENT	APPLICATION
Possible Graphic	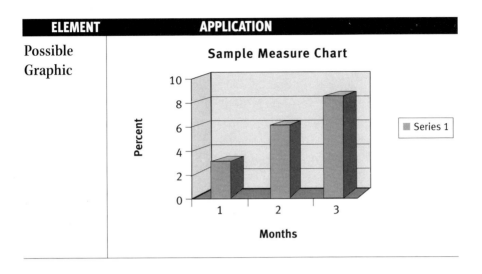

ANALYZING THE DIVERSITY STYLE DIMENSION

The following information provides an overview of the Diversity measures and associated formulas that can be used to monitor the Diversity Style dimension of the organization.

The Diversity Style dimension measures monitor the impact of day-to-day management and leadership behavior which ultimately reflects a picture of the organization's climate (what its like to work here) and the style that creates that climate. If work force diversity is to be successful, it must be utilized, managed and appreciated.

Style Measure-1

ELEMENT	APPLICATION
Measure	Stratified Focus Group Feedback Benchmarks

ELEMENT	APPLICATION
Measure Description	Focus groups are a powerful techniques to acquire anecdotal information about the diversity change process that can serve as an early warning system regarding management and leadership issues. Although focus groups can be used for additional things, assessing the Diversity Style dimension is simply one area of focus.
Formula Elements	There is no formula for this measure, however, focus groups usually are conducted in groupings of 8 to 15, selected employees on the basis of the same gender, ethnicity, and position level. The group moderator preferably is of the same ethnicity and gender. Structured 2 to 3 hour sessions can unearth the passion that surrounds some issues, and the "why" behind a numerical answer that may appear on a survey that assesses Diversity Style. The session may also be used to involve employees in structuring solutions to issues they have identified.

Using "content analysis" techniques such as an Affinity diagram method, you can organize the comments you get by categories using a computer database or simple 3x5 cards. If you use 3x5 cards, some of the basic steps include the following:

1. Write each focus group comment on a separate card and place them in a stack.
2. Sort the comments into key issue categories such as communications, gender issues, ageism, etc. (the primary and secondary dimensions of diversity are a good starting place for categorization).
3. Get others to review the data and validate that the correct categories are in place based upon the data shown.
4. Compare these issues with historical or other appropriate benchmarks.

ELEMENT	APPLICATION
	5. Summarize the findings and outline the implications for improvement.
	6. Create action plans for change.
	7. Implement, monitor, measure, and feedback results.
Important Considerations	**Advantages** • Captures "heat" as well as light on issues. • Sends powerful messages about the organization's interest in that group's input. • Involvement of employees in problem solving generates useful input and helps manage expectations. **Disadvantages** • Can be expensive on a per-participant basis. • Its important to be wary of potential bias of focus group moderators. • Can degenerate into grip session if not properly planned and facilitated. • Requires strong logistical support to assure you have the right participants, at the right place, at the right time and matched with the right focus group leader.

Style Measure-2

ELEMENT	APPLICATION
Measure	**% Favorable responses on Organizational Culture Audit (or similar instruments)**
Measure Description	This measure reflects changes in work force opinions and perceptions of Diversity Style and other dimensions.

ELEMENT	APPLICATION
Suggested Use/Purpose	This measure can be used as an early warning system for developing issues and be used to avert turnover, EEO charges, which in turn reduce costs.
Formula Elements	This assessment can be conducted by totaling all of the individual employees responses that indicate an "agree" or "strongly agree" on the survey for each question. Next, compare this aggregate score for each question against historical data to identify gains and losses in each question or survey dimension area. Use the simplest statistics possible. Use simple descriptive statistics, mean, mode, median, range, standard deviation, charts, graphs and tables. It is often helpful to display the statistics in the same format as the questionnaire used. This allows the data to be reviewed in the same context as the initial document used.

Style Measure-3

ELEMENT	APPLICATION
Measure	**Number and Percent of Minorities and Women in Key Management and Leadership.**
Measure Description	This measure reflects changes in the number and percent of minorities and women who are in key management and leadership positions.
Suggested Use/Purpose	This measure can be used as a means to track the progress of minorities and women in key management and leadership positions. Changes in these numbers may signal forward and reverse trends in diverse work force promotional changes.

ELEMENT	APPLICATION
Formula Elements	$\text{N/PMW} = \dfrac{\text{PF}}{\text{LP}} \times 100$ Where: • N/PMW = number and percentage of minorities and women in key leadership positions. • PF = number of leadership positions filled with minorities and/or women (*e.g.*, 19) • LP = number of leadership positions (*e.g.*, 65)
Example	$\text{N/PMW} = \dfrac{19}{65} \times 100$ $= \quad .2923 \quad \times 100$ $= \quad 29.2\%$
Key Analysis or Processing Questions Examine for this Measure	1. What is the number? 2. How does this number compare by department, division, or region? 3. How does this figure compare with others in our industry? Our competition? 4. What are the business implications and consequences of this number based upon the organization's strategic objectives? 5. What should our next steps be in light of this information? Why? When? Who? How? What Barriers exist?

Style Measure-4

ELEMENT	APPLICATION
Measure	**Five-by-Five Study - 5 years at level 5 performance**
Measure Description	This measure reflects a comparative analysis of the promotional trend(s) present in the organization between employee groups.

ELEMENT	APPLICATION
Suggested Use/Purpose	This measure can be used to track the promotional progress of primary group employees versus those in the diverse work group population. This measure is based upon the premise that the organization should be interested in the growth and development of its high performers over time. It seeks to examine the level of comparable career progress made by diverse work group employees and maintaining equity amongst all groups. High performers are defined here as employees with performance ratings of 5 or 6 on a 6-point scale.
Formula Elements	The term "5-by-5 study" refers to the method of tracking 5-rated (or 6) performers in both groups over a period of 5 years and comparing results between groups such as: • Salary progression (merit-pay raises, compa-ratios, position within salary range after this period, etc.) • Benefits and Incentives Offered (stock options, relocation allowances, relocation reimbursements allowed versus those denied, home buying program offered, Cost-of-Living Allowance (COLA) computed, pension plans offered, special memberships offered, etc.) • Promotion Rate • Job Level and position within the organization • Span of Control • Task Force assignment opportunities • Mentoring Relationships (formal or informal) • Formal Inclusion in Succession Plan • Etc. You can choose as many dimensions as you like to compare. Usually, selecting a "top-ten list" can keep the study focused. At any rate, these measures should be part of the key benchmarks tracked by the organiza

ELEMENT	APPLICATION
	tion to gauge its performance and human asset utilization.
	Most of these comparisons can be made by using a matrix worksheet to examine and compare the groups by category of measure (see 5-by-5 worksheet). However, be careful not to lump groups using averages only. A 5-by-5 study usually examines the data on a "person-by-person" basis within a group, then drawing conclusions. Once considered, this information should suggest that, all things being equal, high performers in all groups examined have progressed at relatively the same pace, been treated fairly, and have been effectively utilized by the organization.
Example	**See 5-by-5 Worksheet**
Key Analysis or Processing Questions Examine for this Measure	1. What are the numbers and results? 2. What are the percentage and actual number gaps between years between groups (*i.e.*, comparing or calculating differences in year 1 for group 1 with year 1 for group 2)? 3. How do these numbers compare by department, division, or region? 4. What are the business implications and consequences of the numbers based upon the organization's strategic objectives? 5. What should our next steps be in light of this information? Why? When? Who? How? What Barriers exist?

	FIVE-BY-FIVE STUDY WORKSHEET									
	Group 1					Group 2				
Measure / Years	YR1	YR2	YR3	YR4	YR5	YR1	YR2	YR3	YR4	YR5
Salary Progression										
•Merit Pay Increase (%)										
•Compa-ratio										
•Position within Range										
Benefits & Incentives Offered										
•Stock Options										
•Relocation Allowance										
•COLA										
•Etc.										
Promotion Rate										
•Promo Period (#Mos)										
•Title										
Job Level										
•% in 1st Level Supv.										
•% in 2nd Level Mgt										
• % in Executive Level										
Span of Control										
•Avg. # Direct Reports										
Task Force Assignment										
•# Assignments During Period										
Mentoring Relationships										
•# Formal										
•# Informal										
Inclusion in Succession Plans										
•# in plan										
•# not in plan										

Style Measure-5

ELEMENT	APPLICATION
Measure	$ and % of Budget Allocated to Diversity Initiatives
Measure Description	This measure reflects changes in the dollars and percent of budget that is allocated to diversity initiatives.
Suggested Use/Purpose	Using budget as one indicator of the perceived importance of an organizational activity, this measure can be used to track the diversity initiative's perceived value relative to other strategic objectives. Changes in this number relative to changes in other organizational activities can lend some perspective to how its contribution is perceived.
Formula Elements	• Diversity budget this year (DB) • Budget for other key strategic departments (Marketing, Sales, Operations, etc. (MKTG, SLS, OPN, etc.) • % of total organizational budget (%TOTBUD)
Example	**Total Budget = $50,000,000** **DB** = $ 200,000 **%TOTBUD** = .4% **MKTG** = $5 Million **%TOTBUD** = 10% **SLS** = $8 Million **%TOTBUD** = 16%
Key Analysis or Processing Questions Examine for this Measure	1. What are the numbers? 2. How do the numbers compare by department? By year? 3. How do these figures compare with others in our industry? Our competition? 4. What are the business implications and consequences of these numbers based upon the organization's strategic objectives? 5. What should our next steps be in light of this information? Why? When? Who? How? What Barriers exist?

Style Measure-6

Mentoring Analysis

This measure reflects the organization's approach to supporting an employee's professional development. Partly as a response to the possibility that mentoring may not be as accessible to non-majority group members, some organizations have created formal mentoring programs. In some cases these programs are available to all employees and in others they are targeted for members of diverse work groups that have been found to be excluded or disadvantaged in normal, informal mentoring activity. In formal mentoring programs, organizations facilitate the matching of mentors and proteges. They do so in a variety of ways, ranging from hosting social events at which mentors and proteges can meet and pursue matches of mutual interest on their own to assigning mentors to specific proteges.

According to Taylor Cox, Jr., author of Cultural Diversity in Organizations, some experts believe that assigned mentoring does not work well. Cox recommends the following guidelines:

- Do not use formal mentoring unless explicit data indicate a need for it. The same principle applies to targeted mentoring programs.

- Use assigned mentors only as a last resort: maximize voluntary matches first.

- If mentors are assigned, make them preliminary assignments with review after six months and the possibility of reassignment or termination of participation in the program.

In addition to the above, scholars indicate several principles that should be followed to increase effectiveness:

- Select mentors carefully to ensure that they are genuinely committed and good at development.

- Involve proteges in creating matches

- Provide organizational incentives for being a mentor.

- Provide training for both mentors and proteges.

- Establish some formal mechanism to monitor progress of the relationships and to evaluate their effectiveness.

To assess the effectiveness of the mentor in the organizational mentoring process, it may be helpful to evaluate them using the following key criteria which was adapted from Gardenswartz and Rowe:

- **Diversity and Cultural Knowledge**—How much does the mentor know about diversity and the culture of the protege? How well does the mentor embrace these ideas and people from other cultures?

- **Coaching Support**—Is the mentor a cheerleader for the protege. Does he/she offer encouragement, support risk-taking and selling oneself or one's ideas?

- **Usefulness of Feedback**—Does the mentor give the protege usable corrective and supportive information based upon behaviors seen firsthand?

- **Teaching Accountability** — Does the mentor help explain the importance of cause and effect and the notion of consequences of behavior? Does the mentor help the protege almost always see and create options?

- **Imparting Big Picture Thinking**—Does the mentor help the protege generate broad perspectives of view to see issues from various sides? Does the mentor help the protege see both the macro and micro view, make their choices, and then live with the results?

- **Teaching Promotability Skills**—Does the mentor understand how the protege learns and thinks? Does the mentor have sensitivity to the customs and subtle but significant nuances of the protege? Does the mentor understand what adaptation may be required for promotion and where certain behaviors cross the line to career destruction?

- **Creating Collaborative Partnerships**—Does the mentor help the protege develop goals? Does the mentor teach the protege about the unwritten rules of the organization to build relationships and retain the ability to be politically astute? Does the mentor serve as the protege's professional confidante?

Based upon this list of criteria, the assessment form on the following page can be used to gauge how well the mentor is assisting the protege.

MENTORING ANALYSIS

***Direction**: Circle the number which reflects your view of your coach/mentor.*

Diversity and Cultural Knowledge	1 Limited/No Knowledge	2	3	4	5 Very Knowledgeable

Coaching Support	1 Little/No Support	2	3	4	5 Full Support
Usefulness of Feedback	1 Not Useful	2	3	4	5 Very Useful
Teaches Accountability	1 No Training	2	3	4	5 A Lot of Training
Teaches Big Picture Thinking	1 No Training	2	3	4	5 A Lot of Training
Teaches Promotability Skills	1 No Training	2	3	4	5 A Lot of Training
Creates Collaborative Partnerships	1 Little/No Collaboration	2	3	4	5 A Lot of Collaboration

The measures presented here are just a small sampling of the variety of diversity staffing and style (or cultural) measures that can be used. The diversity staff and style dimensions of the Diversity 9-S Framework are vital links in the systematic change process to build a more inclusive work environment. If the organization is to be successful in utilizing diverse workforce assets, staff members must be recruited and retained, and a culture must exist that allows all employees to achieve their potential in pursuit of organizational objectives.

CHAPTER 10 Conclusion: The Strategic Advantage of Diversity

CONTRIBUTING TO THE BOTTOM-LINE

Something I mentioned earlier certainly bears repeating before closing out this first volume. If it were easy to measure diversity results, many more people would be doing this as a matter of routine. However, there is distance still to be traveled and much to be learned.

There may be some who would agree and disagree with the measures and methods suggested in this book. I accept all suggestions and criticisms for changes and expansion of the ideas and approaches covered. In fact, I welcome them in order to begin a serious dialogue and to initiate research into the further study of diversity measurement. I am already working on volume two of Measuring Diversity Results with additional measures and more advanced measurement processes. Diversity has an inordinate amount of value to contribute to organizational performance, especially if its contributions are tracked and managed.

> **If it were easy to measure diversity results, many more people would be doing this as a matter of routine.**

It is my opinion that for the most part technology is non-competitive. That is, you can take two identical buildings, equip them with identical technology, and staff them with similar groups of diverse people. Depending on how these diverse people resources are supported, utilized and managed within the organization, one facility will certainly out perform the other. A major element in this performance factor difference will lie in how effectively the organization used these diverse resources in a systematic way as a strategic advantage in concert with technology.

By using approaches such as the Diversity 9 - S Framework and the assessment methodologies and tools contained in this book, you can frame your diversity initiatives and their contributions to demonstrate this competitive difference in more concrete terms. The Diversity 9 - S Framework provides a systematic method for organizing the diversity assessment processes in line with proven organizational change strategies. When all nine "S's" are in place, it can create a major cultural shift in the organization. When aligned with organizational objectives, diversity can be a powerful contributor to the organization's competitive advantage.

Managing and measuring the strategic contribution of diverse workforce resources will become mandatory in the future, especially with the advent of new technologies and the need to have people who can create and apply them in our changing global marketplace. The process and outcomes of measuring diversity results can improve an organization's perception of diversity initiatives by producing evidence of real worth to the organization, by linking these initiatives to improved organizational effectiveness, and by changing the relationship with line managers.

It is also necessary to recognize the political nature of diversity measurement. The information produced in an evaluation study is likely to be a source of power. Organizations are usually comprised of groups of people with very different interests whose views on the importance of diversity will vary. Their opinions are often based upon information which is passing informally around the organizational networks. Formal measurement of diversity and the collection of evaluative data can challenge their opinions if this is thought necessary.

The very essence of measurement and evaluation in the way it is described in this book will hopefully change the questions people ask about diversity and its contributions. By changing the questions people ask, changes the way they think. It is my hope that this book has helped you examine some of the theoretical aspects of diversity measurement, but more importantly, I hope it has given you a framework and some step-by-step processes to translate this theory into practice and concrete numbers! When we start to show management exactly how much value diversity efforts can contribute to the process of building an inclusive work environment, improving organizational performance, and achieving business objectives, these initiatives will become a strategic requirement.

Index

—$—

$ and % of Budget Allocated to Diversity Initiatives, 66, 169, 191

—%—

% Favorable responses on Organizational Culture Audit, 66, 168, 185

—A—

Absence Rate, 65, 95, 111-113. See also Absenteeism Cost

Absenteeism Cost, 65, 95, 114. See also Absence Rate

accountability, v, 26-27, 29-30, 60, 96, 108-109, 193, 195

    matrix for 5 year transition process, 108

accuracy, 15, 25-26, 30, 161

Affirmative action, 17, 98, 100

Age-Range Legend, 126

Alignment

    with strategic goals, 14

Applying Diversity Training On-the-Job, 151

Applying Diversity Training On-the-Job: Manager's Version, 154

Appreciating differences, 8

Assessment of Diversity-Related Knowledge, 147

average cost per interview, 40

Average Hourly Rate, 65, 95, 109

Average ROI

    calculation of, 162, 164

Average Tenure By Diversity Grouping versus Former Employees, 66, 168, 177

—B—

base value, 48-49, 89

Baytos, viii, 10, 15-17, 20, 96

benchmarking process, 90

Brainstorming Method, 31

business rationale, 53, 64, 94, 96-101

—C—

CEOs

    and diversity, 13

competitive advantage, 21, 29, 61, 118, 198

control group, 27

Control measures, 43

cost

    evaluation of, 29

Cost Per Diversity Hire, 39, 41, 66, 72, 168-171

Course Evaluation, 138

Creating Formulas, 40

Creativity or Innovation

    measures of, 45

    culture survey, 34

—D—

day care, 20

degree of variation, 64, 94, 103-104, 106-107

    exercise, 43, 103, 139

    exercise #2, 107

dependent variable, 40, 41, 45, 47

direct and indirect

    conversions of, 27

    measures, 26

Diversity

    creating measures for, 31

    Weld research and experimentation, 26

    global competition, 8

    hiring, 41

    line manager perceptions of, 9

    measure accuracy compared to other departments, 25

    measuring up, 15

    uncontrollable variables, 26

Diversity 9-S Framework, iv, viii, 4-5, 53, 55, 57-63, 65, 67, 71-73, 75, 77, 85, 88, 91, 94-95, 167, 169, 195

Diversity 9-S measures

    listing of measures by category, 63

Diversity 9-S Model

    graphic of,56

Diversity Attitude Change, 141

Diversity Hire Performance Impact, 66, 168, 175

Diversity Hire Referral Rate, 66, 168, 174

Diversity Hit Rate, 66, 168, 173

Diversity Knowledge Change, 140

Diversity manager

    accountability for implementation, 1

Diversity Pre- and Post-Course Self-Assessment, 156

Diversity professionals

    fear of measurement, 12

Diversity Role Play Checklist, 147

Diversity Self-Assessment, 144, 146

Diversity Skill (Behavior) Change, 141

Diversity Stability Factor, Diversity Instability Factor, 66, 168, 179

Diversity Survival Rate, Diversity Loss Rate, 181

Diversity trainer, 1

Diversity Values Written, 64, 70, 82

Diversity Vision/Mission Written, 63, 70, 73

During the course, 134, 139

—E—

EEO, 18-19, 186

Effect of Absenteeism on Labor Utilization, 95, 117

effective, 2, 21, 23

efficient, 23

End of course, 134, 139

Evaluation, 129

exclusion

   types of, 36

—F—

Family of Measures, 31, 43, 46, 48, 50, 64, 71, 88-90

Family of Measures Method, 31, 43, 48, 64, 71, 88-90

financial return, 43

Five-by-Five Study, 187, 190

Five-by-Five Study Worksheet, 190

—G—

Gardenswartz, vii, 103, 193

Gross Productivity Percent vs. Prior Three Years, 79

guiding and daily beliefs, 57

—H—

human capital plan, 59

—I—

Immediate transfer, 149

independent variables, 34, 39, 41

indirect measure, 24

inflation, 28

—J—

Jack Phillips, 130

—K—

Kirkpatrick, Donald, 130

Kirkpatrick Skills Evaluation Model Plus, 130

—L—

language of business, iii, 6, 30

Layoffs, 13

Level 3, 62, 130-133, 148-149, 156, 158

Level 1, 130, 132, 134-137, 139

Level 2, 130-132, 137, 139-140

Level 4, 131, 133, 157-158, 161

Level 5, 66, 131, 133, 158, 161, 169, 187

—M—

Manager's Post-Training Evaluations, 150

Matrix Method, 31, 33-34, 40

Measurement Matrix, 34, 36

mental model

   measures, 59

Mentoring, 21, 42, 62, 66, 169, 188, 190, 192-194

Mentoring Analysis, 66, 169, 192, 194

   key criteria for, 195

   principles for, 195

Mentoring Analysis Survey, 196

minorities, 17-19, 21, 47-48, 63, 66, 89, 99, 159, 168, 186-187

minority/female, 179

—N—

NGT, 32

Nominal Group Technique, 31-32, 34

Number and Percent of Minorities and Women in Key Management and Leadership, 186

Number and type of policies and procedures assessed for diverse workforce impact, 95, 122

Number and type of policies and procedures changed to support diversity, 95, 122

Number of Diverse Work Teams by Strategic Result Area, 94, 105

Number of Times Diversity Business Rationale Mentioned as a Strategy, 94, 100

Number of Times Diversity Mentioned as a Strategy, 74, 83, 94, 100

Number of Times Diversity Values Mentioned as a Strategy, 83

Numbers

   how management uses them, 2

   no escaping them, 2

—O—

Objectives Matrix, 46, 48, 88

One to three months after training, 149

Open-Ended questions, 135-136, 139

Organizational Impact Evaluation, 159

Organizational Results, 1, 131, 133, 157-160, 168

Organizational Results Survey, 158-159, 168

Outcome

   measures of, 55

—P—

partial measures, 25

Participant Post-Training Surveys, 149

Percent Change in Local or Global Customer Diversity Demographics vs Past 3-5 Years, 75

Index

Percent Change in Local or Global Employee Diversity Demographics vs. Past 3-5 Years, 77

Percent Diversity Values Training Completed, 70, 84

Percentage of Diversity Goals Completed, 101-102

Percentage of Diversity Turnover by Performance Level, 123

Percentage of Gender-Based Pay Differential, 120

Performance Change, 156-157

Performance Checklist for Diversity Training Transfer, 155

Performance Rating, 126, 155-156, 175

Peter Drucker, 24

Planning measures, 43

Policy Tracking Worksheet, 123

precision, 5, 23, 25-27, 29-30

Pretest, 140

productive
    productivity and measurement, 23

Productivity
    measures of, 44

profitability, 7, 25, 26, 50, 97, 99, 162, 163

—Q—

Quality
    measures of, 45

—R—

Rating scales,, 135-136, 142-143

Reactions to Diversity Training, 137

Recruiter, 36-38, 41, 182

Reduced costs, 9, 18-19, 28

Reduced expenses, 18

Reengineering, 13, 15

report card, 27, 29, 59

type of measures, 45

Return on Training Investment, 129, 158, 161

ROA and ROE, 164

ROI, 65, 88, 161-162, 164-165

Rowe, vii, 103, 193

—S—

Sample Business Rationale for Diversity Initiatives, 98-99

Satisfaction with Diversity Training Course Effectiveness, 152

savings, 28-29, 161, 164

Screening measures, 44

Shared Values, 5, 57, 64, 66, 69-71, 73, 75, 77, 79, 81-85, 87, 89, 91, 93

Shared Vision, 5, 57, 63, 66, 69-71, 73-75, 77, 79, 81, 83, 85, 87, 89, 91, 93, 96

Shortly after the course, 135

Skills, 1, 5, 54, 59, 61-62, 65, 84-85, 87, 93, 99, 127, 129-133, 135, 137, 139, 141, 143, 145, 147-151, 153-159, 161, 163, 165, 194-195

Society for Human Resources Management, 10

Staff, 5, 18, 62, 66, 167-169, 171, 173, 175, 177, 179, 181, 183, 185, 187, 189, 191, 193, 195

Standards, 5, 17, 53, 58, 64, 66, 69, 71, 73, 75, 77, 79, 81, 83, 85-89, 91, 93, 102, 110, 114, 116, 176, 179-180, 182

statistical significance, 26

statistics, iii, 26, 33-34, 63, 76, 78, 123-124, 135, 186

strategic goals, 33

Strategy, 5, 15, 59, 63-64, 66, 70, 74-75, 83, 91, 93-97, 99-101, 103, 105, 107, 109, 111, 113, 115, 117, 119, 121, 123, 125, 127

Stratified Focus Group Feedback Benchmarks, 168, 183

Structure, 5, 53, 55, 60, 64, 66, 91, 93-95, 97, 99, 101, 103, 105-109, 111, 113, 115, 117, 119, 121, 123-125, 127

Style, 5, 62, 66, 87, 93, 139, 167-169, 171, 173, 175, 177, 179, 181, 183-187, 189, 191-193, 195

Subjectivity myth, 11-12

Survey Rating of Values Installation, 64, 70, 85

system for installing accountability, 108

Systems, 5, 53, 55, 58, 60, 65-66, 91, 93-97, 99, 101, 103, 105, 107-109, 111, 113-115, 117, 119-123, 125, 127

—T—

Taylor Cox, vii, 10, 45, 192

Time-to-Fill, 28, 66

Top management, 12, 16, 53, 57

Training Evaluation Measures, 5, 129, 131, 133, 135, 137, 139, 141, 143, 145, 147, 149, 151, 153, 155, 157, 159, 161, 163, 165

Transfer of Training, 148, 156

turnover, 17-21, 27, 47, 88, 99, 111, 123, 126, 178-179, 186

Types of Skill Development Measures, 130

—U—

Utilization
    measures of, 45

—V—

value chain, 27-28

Variations, 136

—W—

Wall Street, 14, 20-21

whole and partial measures, 25

whole measures, 25, 42

workforce utilization, 22, 105

Writing of Diversity Business Rationale, 100

References

Albert, Kenneth J. *How to Solve Business Problems*. New York: McGraw-Hill. 1978.

Bader, Gloria E, Bloom, Audrey E., Chang, Richard Y. *Measuring Team Performance*. Irvine California: Richard Chang Associates Inc. 1994.

Bader, Gloria E., Bloom, Audrey E. *Make Your Training Results Last*. Irvine California: Richard Chang Associates Inc. 1994.

Baytos, Lawrence M. *Designing & Implementing Successful Diversity Programs*. New Jersey: Prentice Hall. 1995.

Bramley, Peter. *Evaluating Training Effectiveness: Translating Theory into Practice*. London: McGraw-Hill. 1991.

Casio, Wayne F. *Applied Psychology in Personnel Management, Second Edition*. Reston Virginia: Reston Publishing Company, Inc. 1982.

Casio, Wayne F. *Costing Human Resources: The Financial Impact of Behavior in Organizations, Second Edition*. Boston, Massachusetts: PWS-Kent Publishing Company. 1987.

Chang, Richard Y., Kelly, P. Keith. *Improving Through Benchmarking*. Irvine California: Richard Chang Associates Inc. 1994.

Christopher, William F., Thor, Carl G. *Handbook for Productivity Measurement and Improvement*. Portland, Oregon: Productivity Press. 1993.

Cox, Taylor Jr. *Cultural Diversity In Organizations*. San Francisco, California: Berrett-Koehler Publishers. 1993.

Craig, Robert L. *The ASTD Training & Development Handbook: A Guide To Human Resources Development*. New York: McGraw-Hill. 1996.

Edwards, Mark R., Ewen, Ann J. *360° Feedback*. New York: AMACOM. 1996.

Fitz-enz, Jac. *How To Measure Human Resources Management, Second Edition*. New York: McGraw-Hill, Inc. 1995.

Fitz-enz, Jac. *How To Measure Human Resources Management*. New York: McGraw-Hill Book Company. 1984.

Gardenswartz, Lee, Rowe, Anita. *Diverse Teams at Work: Capitalizing on the Power of Diversity*. Chicago: Irwin Professional Publishing. 1994.

Gardenswartz, Lee, Rowe, Anita. *Managing Diversity: A Complete Desk Reference*. New York: Irwin Professional Publishing. 1993.

Gentile, Mary C. *Managerial Excellence Through Diversity*. Chicago: Irwin Professional Publishing. 1996.

Henerson, Marlene E., Morris, Lynn Lyons, Taylor Fitz-Gibbon, Carol. *How To Measure Attitudes*. Newbury Park, California: Sage Publications. 1987.

Hubbard, Edward E. *The Hidden Side Of Resistance To Change*. Petaluma, California: Global Insights Publishing. 1994.

Jackson, Susan E. and Associates. *Diversity in the Workplace*. New York: The Guilford Press. 1992.

Jamieson, David, O'Mara, Julie. *Managing Workforce 2000: Gaining the Diversity Advantage*. San Francisco, California: Jossey-Bass. 1991.

Jerome, Paul J. *Re-Creating Teams During Transitions*. Irvine California: Richard Chang Associates Inc. 1994.

King, Jean A, Morris, Lynn Lyons, Taylor Fitz-Gibbon, Carol. *How To Assess Program Implementation*. Newbury Park, California: Sage Publications. 1987.

McCoy, Thomas J. *Compensation and Motivation*. New York: AMACOM. 1992.

References

Moran, Linda, Musselwhite, Ed, Zenger, John H. *Keeping Teams On Track*. Chicago, Illinois: Irwin Professional Publishing. 1996.

Office of Human Resources, Federal Aviation Administration. *Diversity Training Evaluation Toolkit*. Oklahoma City, Oklahoma: Mike Monroney Aeronautical Center. June, 1994.

Phillips, Jack J. *Handbook of Training Evaluation and Measurement Methods, Second Edition*. Houston, Texas: Gulf Publishing Company. 1991.

Sloma, Richard S. *How To Measure Managerial Performance*. New York: MacMillan Publishing Co., Inc. 1980.

Spencer, Lyle M. Jr. *Calculating Human Resource Costs and Benefits: Cutting Costs and Improving Productivity*. New York: John Wiley & Sons. 1986.

Taylor Fitz-Gibbon, Carol , Morris, Lynn Lyons. *How To Analyze Data*. Newbury Park, California: Sage Publications. 1987.

Thiederman, Sondra. *Bridging Cultural Barriers for Corporate Success*. Lexington, Massachusetts: Lexington, Books. 1991.

Thomas, R, Roosevelt, Jr. *Redefining Diversity*. New York: AMACOM. 1996.

Wade, Pamela A. *Measuring The Impact Of Training*. Irvine California: Richard Chang Associates Inc. 1994.

Zemke, Ron, Thomas Kramlinger. *Figuring Things Out*. Reading Massachusetts: Addison-Wesley Publishing Company, Inc. 1987.